THE AGE-PROOF GARDEN

101 PRACTICAL IDEAS AND PROJECTS FOR STRESS-FREE, LOW-MAINTENANCE SENIOR GARDENING, SHOWN STEP BY STEP IN MORE THAN 500 PHOTOGRAPHS

Patty Cassidy

With special photography by Mark Winwood

southwater

This edition is published by Southwater,
an imprint of Anness Publishing Ltd, Blaby Road, Wigston,
Leicestershire LE18 4SE

info@anness.com
www.southwaterbooks.com; www.annesspublishing.com

If you like the images in this book and would like to
investigate using them for publishing, promotions or
advertising, please visit our website
www.practicalpictures.com

Publisher: Joanna Lorenz
Editorial director: Helen Sudell
Project editor: Emma Clegg
Designer: Andrew Barron
Special photography: Mark Winwood
Additional photography: Heather Hawksford
    and Lynn Keddie
Stylist: Penny Cooke
Illustrator: Liz Pepperell
Production controller: Wendy Lawson

© Anness Publishing Ltd 2012

Previously published as part of a larger volume,
The Illustrated Practical Guide to Gardening for Seniors

PUBLISHER'S NOTE
The author and publishers have made every effort to ensure
that all advice and instructions contained within this book
are accurate and safe, and cannot accept liability for any
errors or omissions that may have been made, nor for any
inaccuracies, nor for any loss, harm or injury that comes
about from following instructions or advice given here.
If you do have any special needs or problems, consult your
doctor or another health professional. Any health advice in
this book cannot replace medical consultation and should
be used in conjunction with professional recommendations.

CONTENTS

INTRODUCTION

I can't remember a time when I didn't garden. One of my earliest memories, in fact, is of planting a row of green bean seeds in a small patch of dirt while my mother hung out the washing. My mother was not much of a gardener, but she was as thrilled as I was when we later discovered the first small sighting of green pushing up through the soil, shaded by the clothes flapping on the line.

ABOVE *Tending a garden is a much-loved pastime and a way to stay healthy, happy and vigorous as we age.*

The chances are that you have had at least one special garden in your lifetime that you cared for, and derived a great deal of joy from as you worked the soil and grew the plants. However large or small, gardens keep us connected with the seasons and with the life cycles of all sorts of living things, including ourselves.

These intangible benefits of gardening are not ones that we have to forfeit as we age, though we may have to learn to adapt our spaces, our tools and our techniques to accommodate changing circumstances. This is written to provide an uplifting and positive view of the normal ageing process and encourage all seniors to get, or stay, involved with the wonderful, life-giving activity of gardening.

AGE-PROOF GARDENS

This book is about gardens that will suit senior gardeners. Rather than categorizing 'seniors' by a specific age, I think of seniors as those of us who have the maturity and wisdom to recognize that we will have to make compromises and adjustments if we want to continue having a positive relationship with gardening.

As we age, the main issues that affect us are to do with our garden environment and our health or energy level. Retirement often means more time to work in the garden and less energy to do it, and balancing the two is a challenge. It may be necessary to reduce gardening chores by getting outside help, re-designing a space or adopting new techniques and tools.

For those moving from a house and garden to another living situation, continuing gardening will necessarily entail re-thinking possibilities. However, this can be fun – using containers, growing vertically and being mindful about the seasonal features of plant choices makes gardening an adventure.

Some of you may be concerned with providing opportunities for loved ones or other seniors who can no longer actively garden. For people helping their senior parents make the transition from the family home to an appropriate residential community, I'll be suggesting questions to ask and features to look for.

Finally, changes and transitions can be stressful, but gardening can calm our anxieties, be a physical outlet for energy, and enrich our sense of well-being.

FINDING YOUR WAY AROUND

In the first section, called Your Garden Environment, I discuss the living situations that senior gardeners might find themselves in. This allows you to literally 'ground' yourself by starting with the environment that relates to your circumstances.

The next section, Making Decisions About Your Garden, is intended as an aid to assessing your options and planning your strategies. It includes both practical and aesthetic considerations.

Three chapters follow looking at different types of garden – Flower and Herb Gardens, Fruit and Vegetable Gardens, and Gardens with Adaptable Features. From creating a herb garden to having a few houseplants on a windowsill, each idea is illustrated and the plants identified.

Finally, the Plant Directory categorizes plants by the light exposure they need to survive and thrive. The focus is on plants that are low-maintenance, offer several seasons of botanical interest and that can stimulate several senses.

Use the ideas in this book not as rigid categories, but as inspiration for a garden that will reflect who you are – your personality, your tastes and, yes, your age.

LEFT *There are many specially adapted tools, such as the long-handled bulb planter shown here, that make gardening activities easier.*

RIGHT *Raised beds and wide pathways are two practical design approaches for gardens used by older people.*

YOUR GARDEN ENVIRONMENT

To some, the word 'garden' brings back memories of a childhood flower plot; to others, grandmother's rose garden or the neighbour's abundant vegetables. While it is useful to have a common understanding of what a garden is, each person's space will be unique.

As we age, many factors determine how our garden takes shape. Gardening may be a form of exercise, a way of engaging with the seasons, or just having fun. Or it may become secondary to travelling, grandchildren and new hobbies. Normal ageing – loss of stamina, arthritis, decreased vision and reduced balance – may limit gardening activities. Most importantly, we need to consider how our physical space defines the way we garden.

This chapter identifies broad living situations and gardening environments that seniors may find themselves in. These include a house with a garden, an apartment with a small garden or patio, and communities for active or frail elders with a shared garden, the latter looking at both independent retirement set-ups and assisted-living communities. A final section looks at the role of gardens in the lives of those who need constant nursing care.

OPPOSITE *Every garden is unique and can be adapted to suit its owner – this one has a raised bed with a wide ledge for seated comfort.*

ABOVE *Every member of the family, including your canine companions, can enjoy the garden and fresh air.*

ABOVE *Appreciating flowers and plants is something gardeners at any age never grow tired of doing.*

ABOVE *Sharing the garden and its produce with grandchildren is one of the most valuable gifts we can give them.*

STAYING PUT: GARDENS FOR INDEPENDENT SENIORS

Seniors today are generally healthier and more robust than their counterparts of even 50 years ago. Thanks to regular exercise, good eating habits, and staying socially active, many independent seniors still live in their family homes and maintain their gardens regularly. Here are some ideas that can help seniors stay connected with gardening, but ease some of the more overwhelming tasks.

ABOVE *Make sure that your water source is close by so that you can easily keep the garden well-irrigated.*

GETTING HELP

One way for home gardeners to increase the likelihood that they continue gardening well into their senior years is to make wise decisions about what tasks others could do for them or with them – like a gardening 'coach'. For example, if you can afford it, a weekly lawn service could relieve you of a time-consuming and less-than-creative activity. During certain times of the year there are other maintenance routines that require much time, energy and risk that an ageing, albeit healthy, gardener could hire out. To cite a fairly obvious example, understanding the risks of getting on ladders as we age, and the devastating injuries that can occur by falling, should encourage the home gardener to hire an arborist or other expert to do the elevated and more risky pruning tasks. Other, less routine, tasks that might call for outside help might include one-off construction of yard or garden features – a tool shed, for example, or a raised bed or a level paving surface – that will contribute to the on-going ease and safety of the home gardener's task.

If hiring professional help is beyond the budget, consider giving friends, relatives or neighbours an opportunity to be generous. A half-day potluck lunch work party can produce wonders in the garden and be a fun social event for families and friends.

MAKING CHANGES

It will come as no surprise, except perhaps to the very young, that ageing means making adjustments. Taking care of how we use our bodies now as we go about our normal gardening routines will go far toward ensuring that we continue gardening well into our 70s, 80s and even 90s.

LEFT *Choose the garden tasks that you like to do and that don't deplete your energy. Gathering dahlias for a bouquet is a pleasant way to start the day.*

Kneeling down to weed the in-ground bed can be hard on both the back and knees, and lugging a heavy hose around to the far corners of the yard can take too much valuable energy and time. Understanding what changes can be made in the home garden's daily work schedule may increase the time spent doing more enjoyable things.

RAISED BEDS

Changing your planting areas to raised beds is one way to ensure that your back and knees get relief and that time spent on weeding and deadheading chores will decrease. This needn't be an elaborate undertaking: merely raking soil in a rectangular shape no higher than 20cm (8in) can create a simple raised bed. A more durable raised bed made of safely preserved wood planks and built at a variety of heights can provide the home gardener with space that is accessible, easy on the joints and muscles and far less demanding to maintain. With help, a more elaborate structure can be constructed with a seating cap all around the perimeter.

This feature gives you a place to sit while weeding as well as a place to rest and to enjoy the fruits of your labours. (*See also* pages 90–97.)

WATERING

Having a water tap (spigot) installed closer to your main gardens or, if possible, getting an irrigation system on a timer to keep the beds watered will make your life easier. A good hose cart that is easily wheeled about is a wise purchase, and will also provide safe and easy storage and reduce the chances of tripping over the hose that didn't get put away. It should attach to your water butt, to make the most of rainwater.

PATHS

Finally, the home gardener may realize that some of the existing garden pathways need improvements, or more significant changes, to allow for easier mobility. Installing lights for evening passage, clearing vegetation off the path, and defining the path edges will make your home safer for both you and your senior guests.

ABOVE *Puttering in the greenhouse or potting shed is a great way to prepare for spring seedlings and vegetable starts.*

The key to making changes in your routine is knowing your strengths and acknowledging your limitations. Just as no two gardens are the same, no two gardeners are the same. More to the point, no one gardener is the same at two different stages of life.

BELOW *A raised bed with a wide seating area makes tending beds easier; the paved floor is flat with no tripping dangers.*

BELOW *A wheeled hose cart takes the awkwardness out of manoeuvring the hose around the garden.*

BELOW *There are many options for flat, stable surfaces – this one uses curved paving that follows the path direction.*

DOWNSIZING TO AN APARTMENT GARDEN

Many seniors may decide to leave the family home, dispose of unused furniture and free themselves from time-consuming garden chores – either because they can no longer cope, or because they want to be ready for future problems. However, their love of gardening will remain undiminished. Downsizing to a smaller set-up such as an apartment needn't mean that gardening is a thing of the past. Here are some things that can be helpful.

ABOVE *Moving to a smaller living space may also reduce your garden area, so use containers to increase your options.*

PATIOS, TERRACES AND BALCONIES

If you are keen to maintain your garden activities, albeit in a smaller context, an apartment or condo that offers a small patio, deck or terrace will be the perfect set-up. When researching an apartment, take note of the sun orientation, since having a sunny or shady location will determine your plant selections and how you use the space.

It's best if the garden is directly connected to your living quarters. This is important for your daily enjoyment of the garden and will allow easy and quick access to get outside and potter about. Some apartments and condos have in-ground spaces for beds and surfaces to place containers.

Determine how many containers you can fit or if there is room for a trellis to allow you to maximize your growing area. Hanging baskets can also give an extra dynamic to a small garden space. Finally, is there a space for a small tree? Adding a slow-growing but richly textured evergreen like a Hinoki cypress can offer you beauty and give you some natural privacy. Alternatively, a small deciduous tree that can add seasons of interest to your terrace is a Japanese maple. A balcony may seem limiting in what you can grow but by placing well-designed boxes and hanging baskets, you can create a lush garden of cascading flowering annuals and perennials.

CHOOSING AND USING CONTAINERS

In a patio, terrace, or balcony garden, containers are going to be essential, not just to hold the plants but as basic design features. Generally speaking, buy the largest container you can accommodate and manage easily, since it will require less watering

LEFT *A small terrace garden can provide all you need to feel at home – lots of plants, comfortable seating and easy access to garden beds.*

ABOVE *A small patio or balcony provides a place for reading the morning paper, sipping coffee or watching the birds.*

and allow you to have a wider variety of plants that make a more interesting garden.

Remember that while colourful, artistic containers are attractive, they can be expensive and heavy – even before you add any soil. Take account of your climate – if you get repeated winter frosts, a ceramic container is likely to crack. Semi-flexible synthetic pots work best in cold regions and these will double up as liners. Plant directly into the plastic pot or liner and then place it in the more decorative container to get the benefits of both.

Also on the market now are terracotta-style resin and fibreglass containers that are more reliable in extreme temperatures. They are also lighter, more durable, less expensive and easier to move. Moving a fully planted container without wheeled support can be dangerous if you don't have the strength and stability. If possible, put your containers on moveable trays since you may want to rearrange your patio area. Techniques for moving containers are explored in more detail on pages 120–123.

CREATING SEASONAL INTEREST

Just because your space is smaller, you don't need to forgo having a garden that is attractive all year round. An important strategy when planning a patio or terrace garden is to think about growing a variety of plants that will give you several seasons of attraction and interest. A careful choice of bulbs, annuals and perennials can give you flowers all year round, and you can add a shrub or two with colourful berries or scented winter flowers. Most of these will need little maintenance other than feeding and watering (if they're in containers) – many bulbs, perennials and shrubs will almost take care of themselves, year after year. If possible, locate the winter containers so they are highly visible from the inside – that way you can enjoy them when it's too cold to spend much time outside.

CREATING HEIGHT VARIATIONS

In a smaller outdoor space you may need to use every part of the area to create interest and to make your own garden statement. One idea is to add a trellis to a large container – this is a good way of giving you more growing space, as well as giving height to your small garden area. By placing the trellis to the back of the container you can add layers of plants in front, thereby creating a mini-garden scene. Climbers such as clematis, honeysuckle and three-leaf akebia can be grown on the trellis, and planting two varieties can provide you with blooms for several months.

A trellis can also be used for growing vegetables such as climbing peas, beans and cucumbers. Certain varieties of tomatoes, squash and melons are also well adapted to grow in small and vertical spaces. With a bit of twine or flexible tape, it's easy to coax these plants on to the trellis and use it during the season for support and stability.

Hanging baskets are another useful feature for patios. Pulley systems are available to assist with the raising and lowering of baskets so that watering and grooming can be done at a safe height. Your planting choices will require a balance of colourful blooms, foliage interest and plants that create the core composition as well as those that cascade over the sides. For easy access, you can use a watering wand with a long handle and angled head.

WINDOW BOXES

Not just appropriate to sills, window boxes can also be attached to a terrace or balcony railing. Available in wood, terracotta, synthetic compounds and plastic, they are easily maintained, usually requiring no bending or high stretching. Growing herbs in a sunny window box and in a temperate climate can give you year-round access to fresh culinary treats.

As your garden changes in size and shape, remind yourself that some of the loveliest gardens in the world are grown in small spaces. Think of your garden as an extension of your home – an 'outdoor room' that is inviting and appealing, no matter what the season.

BELOW *The secluded and shady seating area in this garden is created by the house wall and the soft, enclosing foliage.*

COMMUNITY LIVING AND COMMUNITY GARDENS

As the baby boomer generation has aged, the market has responded by creating residential environments to meet the emerging needs of a growing and greying population. These include independent retirement homes, apartments with a community garden, assisted-living communities providing more hands-on backup and, for those needing long-term support and assistance, nursing-home communities.

ABOVE *Keep the joy of gardening in your life wherever you live by making careful choices about your new community.*

RETIREMENT COMMUNITIES FOR ACTIVE SENIORS

These communities are designed for seniors who are independent, physically active, free of the burdens of home ownership and who require little or no staff assistance. Of course, whatever size of plot or garden is available – from a small courtyard to a more spacious garden – it needs to be well maintained. The advantage of many living facilities of this type is that they have a basic level of garden maintenance provided.

NEW OPPORTUNITIES FOR LEARNING

Retirement from the workplace may be disorienting for the energetic senior who thrived on having a schedule, getting things done and working with a team. However, a retirement community can be ideal to channel your competitive drive, still-curious mind and excess energy and leave you more time to devote to individual interests.

One advantage of a retirement community is ready access to others who share your interest in gardening.

Residents are often provided with gardening areas, and may have an organized garden group. This is likely to be composed of like-minded plant people who might have specialist interests to bring. Devising informal competitions, such as who can grow the biggest pumpkin, raise the best rose or produce the most cherry tomatoes, can inspire active gardeners to participate. This interaction and the sharing of fresh food grown locally are meaningful ways to create stronger bonds and a personal sense of well-being.

BELOW *Ensure that there is a private and sheltered place where you can enjoy the garden throughout the seasons and also appreciate the fruits of your efforts.*

BELOW *Sharing a garden creates new friends and a healthy social network.*

ASSISTED-LIVING COMMUNITIES

The goal of assisted-living communities is to help individuals remain as independent as possible, but to offer services that make performing the tasks of daily living easier and safer. While residents have their own self-contained apartments, they can receive a number of services that can include meals, laundry, housekeeping, medication reminders and transportation to and from appointments. These communities often encourage residents to participate in activities programmes, especially gardening groups.

FINDING THE RIGHT PLACE

For gardeners who still want to garden actively, the assisted-living community should provide several things. Smart facility planners and administrators understand that many of their clients will be coming from homes where gardening played an important role. By creating and supporting beautiful grounds, these forward-thinking communities are creating gardens where the residents can have a plot or raised bed to grow plants of their choice. Making sure there are wide, well-lit paths that allow strolling in the gardens will encourage residents to be outdoors. Such gardens will also be designed to accommodate walkers and wheelchairs and will include raised beds, easy and accessible watering options and a supply of adaptive tools.

GETTING YOUR NEEDS MET

A thoughtful assisted-living community will provide a light and airy room where people can gather to discuss their mutual gardening interests and participate in activities. Some homes

RIGHT *Many communities offer plots where flowers and vegetables can be cultivated by a supervised garden group.*

will give the residents an area where they can raise plants and vegetables from seed indoors. This process keeps seniors connected with the cycles of life, and enables the continuation of gardening activities.

Many communities have a horticulture therapist or other specialist who is trained to assist the residents with their gardens, teach horticulture and propagation, and perhaps offer a weekly garden group. When ageing issues limit certain physical chores, the specialist can create an environment in which gardening is still accessible on many levels.

Many such communities will have libraries, or at least a common room with a selection of reading material. If you are lucky, the selection will include many of the books and magazines that have been written about the pleasures of gardening. You probably have your own collection of garden books that you've accumulated over the years. Some of these may be practical how-to books geared to the more active gardener, but others might address

such questions as why we garden, or recount one person's interesting history or journal as a gardener. Reading aloud from these in a group can be a pleasure for all involved. As the Spanish poet Lope de Vega wrote, "With a few flowers in my garden, half a dozen pictures and some books, I live without envy."

OUTINGS AND FIELD TRIPS

Because those who live in assisted-living communities are often able-bodied and mobile, they are able to make trips to local nurseries, arboretums and botanical gardens. Many such locations have naturalists available to give tours and to answer visitors' questions. Choosing these sites so they're accessible to seniors ensures that those with mobility aids such as a wheelchairs or walkers can also participate.

There's no question that assisted-living communities have more limitations than other set-ups, but with imagination and initiative you can turn these limitations into opportunities.

CARING FOR OTHERS

You may be in a situation where you are responsible for a friend or relative who can no longer care for themselves because of their deteriorating physical or cognitive health. In this case a family-care home, a skilled-nursing facility or an Alzheimer's or memory-care community are all options. The goal is to maintain quality of life for residents as their needs change over the course of their disease. In a residential set-up such as this, the garden space can be a defining factor in the quality of life of those who live there.

ABOVE *Well-designed raised beds in communities give residents easy access as well as safe passageways.*

A PROTECTIVE ENVIRONMENT

Adult-care or family-care homes are private residences, staffed and lived in by licensed, trained caregivers who provide their homes for small groups of seniors who need assistance in their daily care. Often, there is a patio or garden where residents can sit in the fresh air and enjoy the sun. When researching adult care homes for your loved ones, ask about the garden facilities to learn what the gardening options are.

A skilled-nursing facility provides a therapeutic and safe environment for an older person. Some residents may be there for a period of rehabilitation; others may be there for long-term care. These nursing facilities offer a range of activities that meet the social, physical and emotional needs of the residents. While the level of involvement in gardening will inevitably change at this stage of life, gardens and the natural world have many benefits and an enlightened facility will provide various gardening and outdoor opportunities. Often a horticultural therapist is available, either in a weekly group or offering one-to-one support to those who are interested.

Increasingly available now are Alzheimer or memory-care communities. These residential homes strive to maintain a rich and appropriate quality of life for those who live there as their physical and psychological needs change over the course of their disease. Many have horticultural therapy programmes, which are very beneficial to this special group of seniors – they help to keep these people engaged with life, connected to others and to the natural world around them.

GROUP ACTIVITIES

Gardening groups have much to offer nursing-care residents. Activities will be seasonally based, designed around residents' requirements. A skilled horticultural therapist will adapt their sessions to meet the needs of the group, or of an individual who may be having a difficult time. For those with memory problems, developing a rapport with each resident and knowing something about their past will help to trigger a memory or relate a story so that they feel respected and connected. Another method is to pass around plants and natural materials that each resident can explore.

While those with dementia can be unpredictable in a group, positive interaction will increase as experiences, gardening stories and memories are shared. With these come laughter, a sense of fun and a mutual respect.

Finding care communities for your loved ones that provide such activities is not always easy, but it will become more so as the benefits of horticultural therapy become better understood and appreciated. Pass the word.

LEFT *Whether you are active or have limited energy, a few quiet moments in the garden can be therapeutic and restorative.*

ABOVE *A garden with a diversity of plants will stimulate the five senses and get people to experience nature in new ways.*

ABOVE *The sweet fragrance of garden flowers keeps you in touch with the addictive pleasure of gardens.*

RESTORATIVE GARDENS

Having an accessible, well-designed, multi-seasonal garden in a nursing-care community allows residents to be in a safe and secure setting while getting fresh air, sunshine and exercise. For many, simply sitting in a chair with a view into the garden can be a comforting and therapeutic experience and provides another connection to the passing of the seasons. Attracting wildlife such as birds and butterflies gives another connection to the natural world. What is more, plantings of old-fashioned flowers with sensory features will stimulate memories.

Research has shown that while many people with Alzheimer's cannot remember what happened only moments earlier, their recollection of events from years ago is unusually strong. The sense of smell may be diminished with Alzheimer's disease, but the sense of touch seems to stay intact. As the actress Helen Hayes wrote in her later years: "I dig my fingers deep into the soft earth. I can feel its energy, and my spirits soar."

These insights are important for planners and staff, but also for those visiting loved ones. Doing something together rather than trying to force a conversation can be a relief to visitor and resident alike. Alzheimer's research has shown that even the simple act of taking your loved one out in a garden creates a focal point for mutual attention and conversation. While most memory-care residents cannot actively garden, they can use small watering cans so that they can irrigate the pots and containers. With one-to-one contact, a horticulture therapist or a visitor can help a resident do some simple weeding or deadheading.

RECEPTIVE GARDENING

The motivation for active gardening, and the opportunity to do so, is minimal when residing in either a skilled-nursing or memory-care community. This is where receptive gardening, or enjoying the fruits of others' labours, comes into play. As we already know, just being around beautiful plants is a great motivator for maintaining people's

strength and enthusiasm. What's more, a daily half-hour dose of sunlight on the face and forearms replenishes vitamin D and promotes skeletal health. Even sitting indoors with a view into the garden can be a comforting experience. Contact with plants or flowers will help keep spirits high, and is especially beneficial for bed-ridden patients.

Any good therapeutic garden will track the cycles of life and the passing of the seasons. Spring blooms on tulips, summer sunflowers, colourful foliage in the autumn, and a beautiful evergreen in winter can orientate residents to the pattern of nature's cycles. Simple techniques such as having a peanut feeder near the windows will give a close view of the garden bird life. Another idea is to make dried corncobs and suet available in the winter months – this will attract squirrels and seed-eating birds.

BELOW *If it is difficult to go into the garden, an attractive window view brings the charm of the garden inside.*

MAKING DECISIONS ABOUT YOUR GARDEN

The most enjoyable decisions we make in our garden are likely to be the choice of summer flowers for planting, what vegetable seeds to sow or which new tree to add. However, many other more nuts-and-bolts factors come into play when you are, for example, remodelling an existing bed or getting a feel for a new garden.

The light exposure, the soil type and texture, the amount of rainfall and the climate zone are some of the practical essentials covered here that you need to understand if you're to have a successful garden. Low-maintenance plants and those that appeal to the five senses will involve seniors to the full, both in the management and enjoyment of gardens, and the ideas included here open up possibilities for a beautiful, easy-to-care-for environment full of sensory surprises. As you read this chapter, think about how appropriate your decisions are for your physical potential or limitations – that is, how much gardening are you willing and able to deal with? Being practical and honest about this will keep both you and your garden happy and healthy. In most cases, we don't need to stop all gardening, but rather think about making small adjustments to our routines.

OPPOSITE *Think about what you want – buying small potted plants instead of seeds can save you a lot of effort.*

ABOVE *A salad garden composed of mixed greens and lettuces is both beautiful and practical.*

ABOVE *A cutting garden provides you with flowers of all kinds – to enjoy in place or to bring the delights of the garden indoors.*

ABOVE *Pack a container with tulip bulbs in the autumn and wait for a wonderful spring display.*

PRACTICAL CONSIDERATIONS

Deciding what to plant and where to plant it can be like rearranging the living room furniture. Is the sofa too big for this wall? Will sun fade the new upholstery? Do some of the old pieces need replacing? Often the process shifts as you see how the space looks as a permanent fixture. Planting a garden is a similar process. However, given that plants are dynamic, living organisms, creating and maintaining a garden involves even more factors.

ABOVE *You may decide to remove those floppy tall flowers that require staking and replace them with more 'obedient' plants.*

INITIAL ANALYSIS

All gardeners have successes and failures in the planting decisions that they make. Even an experienced gardener sometimes loses a plant, in spite of careful planning.

For senior gardeners, the chances of losing plants and therefore of having disappointments in the garden need to be minimized. The plain fact is that every failed planting means that extra time and energy needs to be spent organizing a replacement. There are, simply, better ways to spend your time. So for those with limited energy, how can you minimize your failures?

The answer is to choose plants that are reliable, and make sure you can give them the right conditions. The material in this book is designed with this in mind, to offer plant suggestions that will give you the best chance of being successful and feeling rewarded for your labours.

FACTORS TO CONSIDER BEFORE MAKING PLANTING DECISIONS

What is the climate?
For many seniors who may relocate in their retirement, perhaps escaping from a harsh winter climate to a warmer, dry environment, a whole new gardening world awaits. Look at the gardens in the area and see which plants are thriving to get reliable planting ideas.

How much space is there?
Downsizing to a small patio or terrace from a family home with trees, beds and a lawn will alter your options.

What is the light exposure?
Knowing if your garden is in full sun, full shade or a combination of both will guide your plant choices.

What is the soil quality?
Learn about the soil composition (clay, sand or loam) as well as its pH value (the balance of acid and alkaline). This will help you select appropriate plants or encourage you to begin the amendment process to improve the quality of your soil.

Watering options?
If the soil is dry and watering is a problem, try to choose plants that can tolerate drought conditions. This also creates a low-maintenance garden – lugging around awkward hoses or heavy watering cans is unsafe and can add stress to joints and muscles.

SOIL CARE

Protect the soil structure by covering it with green manure crops or an organic mulch. This also protects the creatures who live beneath the soil.

FAR LEFT *A rotavator is a labour-reducing method of breaking up the soil to prepare it for planting. They can often be hired.*

LEFT *A well-conditioned soil will pay dividends in terms of enhanced plant growth and development.*

DETERMINING YOUR SOIL TYPE: THE SQUEEZE TEST

You need to know the soil characteristics of your garden so that you can choose the best cultivation technique. Soil is described in different ways, such as heavy, light, sandy, clay, loam, poor or good. For the gardener, there are three types of soil that are important, clay, sand and loam, each with a specific visual and handling quality. Loam is the easiest soil to manage, but you can work on both clay and sandy soils to make them as productive. Remember that some plants actually prefer sand or clay. Take a handful of your soil and gently squeeze it to a ball shape to establish which you have.

Clay soil = a sticky ball
Soil with this quality can easily be formed into a ball. Your soil will be clay if water pools on the soil surface, or it sticks to your boots in winter and dries hard in summer. Clay soil is the most fertile, but can have drainage problems. To improve poorly drained clay, dig in grit and bulky organic matter, such as well-rotted manure or spent mushroom compost (soil mix).

Sandy soil = a hard-to-make ball
This soil will disintegrate when you try to form it into a shape. A light-coloured, free-draining soil, it is constantly thirsty in summer and is the poorest quality soil. It is best to mulch sandy soil like this with manure to make it more moisture retentive and fertile. Do this by covering the surface of the damp soil with a thick mulch of well-rotted manure.

Loam or silt = a crumbly ball
You can form loam into a ball that crumbles under pressure. A mixture of sand and clay, this is the best balanced soil for the gardener and poses few cultivation problems. Loams are usually dark because of their high humus (decayed organic matter) content, but lighter soils can be significantly improved by digging in manure.

ABOVE *If you need to work on wet soil, stand on a plank of wood to ensure it is not compacted and its structure destroyed.*

ABOVE *Dry weather causes clay soils to crack, which can be a benefit as it develops their 'crumb structure'.*

ABOVE *Some plants prefer either clay or sandy soils – the sea holly (Eryngium maritimum) thrives in sand or shingle.*

DETERMINING YOUR SOIL pH

This is a measurement of your soil's acidity (sourness, a measure of below 7.0) or alkalinity (sweetness, a measure higher than 7.0). It will help you decide which plants will thrive in your garden. Most plants prefer a specific pH range – acid, alkaline, or near neutral. Soils with a pH of around 6.5 generally have the most nutrients available and are suitable for the widest range of plants. Purchase soil test kits from nurseries or send soil samples to your local agriculture or horticulture agency.

RIGHT *In order to reduce the acidity of the soil add some lime a few weeks before planting.*

MEASURING YOUR SOIL pH WITH AN ELECTRONIC METER

1 *After loosening several different areas of soil, moisten using rainwater (tap water could give false readings) and allow to soak through the ground.*

2 *Take a sample of the wet soil from the first patch only and place in a clean, dry jar, adding more rainwater if necessary, ready for the reading.*

3 *Always clean and dry the probe on the pH meter first to eliminate the risk of an incorrect reading. Do this between each soil reading.*

4 *Push the probe into the moist soil sample and wait until the needle stops moving. The readout will show how acidic or alkaline each sample is.*

UNDERSTANDING THE LIGHT IN YOUR GARDEN

All plants (with the exception of fungi), from the small fern to the towering maple tree, depend on light. To understand how it affects our plants we need to consider three key features of light – quantity, quality and duration.

You need to understand how much sunlight your garden receives each day and where the bright and dark spots are, especially during the growing season. For most gardens, the sunshine is more intense during the summer and particularly from mid-morning to mid-afternoon than during the rest of the day.

RIGHT *In this garden the morning sun glances off the top of the arbour and lights up the border garden of dahlias and flowering shrubs.*

For many plants, the length of time that light shines on them regulates their rate of flowering and fruit ripening. During the growing season, most fruit, vegetables and herbs require at least 6–8 hours of full sunlight a day. Root crops like beets and carrots will do well with 3–6 hours of partial sun.

Some plants deal well with the cool morning sun while others thrive in warm south-facing rock gardens (Northern Hemisphere) or in north-facing rockeries (Southern Hemisphere). Beware of early morning sun striking plants that are prone to frost damage, such as camellias with their early spring buds – warming up more slowly will reduce the risk of harm.

Because most plants can thrive in partial sun or shade, there are many varieties to choose from. Reputable nurseries label plants with essential information, including light requirements.

ABOVE RIGHT *At midday the patio is in full overhead sunlight and, in the summer, pretty warm. The arbour now has a welcoming patch of noontime shade.*

RIGHT *Another day in the summer garden passes. In the evening the patio and bench are in shade and coolness. The setting sun sends down its last warm rays.*

EXPOSURE TABLE

This will give you a quick and easy reference when diagnosing your garden's exposure and what plants will thrive where.

Exposure	Description	Details	Suggestions
6 or more hours of direct sun	Full sun	Late morning through to late afternoon provides the most intense sunlight	Vegetables, most herbs, stonecrops, succulents, cactus
3–6 hours of direct sun	Partial sun or partial shade	In the morning or early afternoon the sun will be diffused through high canopies of shading trees	Most woodland and understorey plants
2 hours or less of direct sunlight	Full shade	The sun is blocked by or heavily filtered through evergreens	Ferns, hostas, camellias, rhododendrons

WORKING AROUND INDIVIDUAL DISABILITIES

Modern medicine and healthier life choices allow today's retirees a greater range of activities and interests. Eventually, however, the physical conditions associated with normal ageing will necessitate some changes in the way that we garden. However, take heart – by knowing our new limitations and adapting our activities accordingly, we can extend the potential of those pleasurable days in the garden.

ABOVE *Arthritis doesn't have to keep you from gardening; discover the tools and plants that will help you stay active.*

ARTHRITIS

Despite medical advances, there are chronic physical conditions that older adults will develop and will need to cope with. Arthritis is the most common of these. It can reduce one's strength, endurance and flexibility. But with adaptive gardening tools, devices and procedures, the senior gardener can stay involved. A wide array of ergonomically designed tools are available to assist you with most garden chores. Cushioned hand grips, adjustable handles, smaller to larger sizing options – all of these can help arthritic gardeners continue their gardening activities.

HYPERTENSION

To prevent or control high blood pressure, one of the most important things we can do is to be physically active. Research shows that gardening is an activity that can help with hypertension as well as reduce our risk of heart disease. To help reduce blood pressure, improve heart health and control diabetes it is suggested that 30 minutes of moderate-level physical activity is advisable almost every day of the week. Power mowing the lawn and raking leaves are both good forms of exercise. With the support of your doctor, gardening can provide you with your own custom-made exercise programme. Think of your garden as your very own private health club!

VISUAL IMPAIRMENTS

Sight is likely to be the first sense that provides us with information about the garden. It is also often the first sense to deteriorate with increasing age. In fact many people notice their sight becoming less acute in their mid- to late forties, and sometimes earlier. Visual impairments usually develop quite slowly and so it's important to pay attention when we feel uncertain about what we're seeing, how we're processing the light or darkness, and how safe we feel negotiating the few steps from the porch.

At first these changes may seem inconsequential, but as time goes on they can be distressing and discouraging. We may begin to have trouble with focus and clarity, become sensitive to glare or lose the ability to discern colours.

In addition, our depth perception can become compromised and we can become confused by changes in levels

FAR LEFT *Stay active by walking in the garden. Your cane can serve as a support as well as a way to explore a flower bed.*

LEFT *Wheelchair-accessible gardens are increasingly common and are popular in retirement communities.*

or surface materials – for example at the back doorstep. Falling or tripping is an undeniable risk, so it is important to think about fine-tuning the garden to ensure maximum safety and security. Installing a small ramp, adding handrails to steps or painting the stairs a contrasting colour are all ways to reduce the risk of falling.

Cataracts can inhibit gardening, but surgery can correct this condition and allow one to resume most activities. For other low-vision issues, such as macular degeneration (compromising the ability to see details), tasks will need to be refined so they're safe as well as satisfying. Storing hoses off pathways in easy and practical carts and always stowing tools away neatly eliminates the danger of tripping and therefore reduces potential accidents. Painting or taping tool handles in a contrasting colour to the ground will make it easier to find them in the garden bed.

SAFETY NOTE

If you notice any changes in your health, you should always consult a physician, particularly concerning your ability to garden.

BALANCE

As we age, our sense of balance is often compromised. There are, however, various ways of making conditions safer where balance is an issue.

Make sure that walking surfaces are smooth and level with good traction, and install a hand rail along main walkways. Grass can be an uneven surface and might throw you off balance, so replace lawns or grassy areas with level paving materials to make movement easier within the garden.

Raising the garden bed will reduce the need to bend over while tending the bed and will also provide a place to sit as you go about your chores. Providing seating in the most frequented spots will allow you to take regular rests. Chairs positioned in shady areas will offer an escape from the sun and a place to sit to enjoy your work – and if they are lightweight they can be moved around easily as the light changes.

LEFT *If you are unsteady on your feet, use a flat and stable surface such as these pavers and tiles to avoid tripping hazards.*

ABOVE *This raised bed is designed to accommodate a gardener in a wheelchair.*

BELOW *Failing eyesight is likely to affect us all – this partially sighted man investigates garden scents with his guide dog.*

WHAT TO PLANT: PERSONAL PREFERENCES

Often, we choose to create a garden based on our early childhood experiences. Helping grandma to plant her sweet peas may forever make you want a few of these growing in your garden. Don't fight it. Apart from evocative garden memories, however, there are contemporary trends, such as growing organic produce or being kind to the environment, that may also influence what we decide to plant.

ABOVE *Grow vegetables that you love to eat, especially those that can be sampled as you harvest them.*

FLOWERS

Because they are showy and attractive, flowers are an essential component of most gardens and often the one that we take the most pride in. They are also valuable in attracting pollinators. Growing plants that have a variety of shapes and heights – the tubular types like fuchsias, the flat-headed varieties like Queen Ann's lace or the open-face disc of tall sunflowers – will provide an accessible entry and landing platform for a variety of bees, flies, butterflies and other beneficial insects.

If you make the right choices you can have flowering plants blooming from the early spring right into the late autumn. Bulbs and tubers, such as daffodils and anemones, can start the early spring garden. Asters and chrysanthemums are great closers to the floral season. And all the flowers in between will grace your garden with their colourful petals.

VEGETABLES

As we learn more about the importance of organic foods in keeping us healthy, creating a vegetable garden becomes ever more appealing. Rule number one when making a vegetable garden is to choose vegetables you really like to eat! While it's fun to look for interesting varieties, make sure you grow the things you're most likely to maintain and harvest. Also, be sure that you make the garden accessible for your particular needs and living situation. Growing beans up a trellis is likely to allow you to harvest more than if you are growing a bush-type bean. Or perhaps a large container with a variety of lettuces and a few potted cherry tomatoes will satisfy your need for fresh salad ingredients.

While vegetable gardening in any form can be incredibly rewarding, remember that there is a considerable amount to plan and to do. Knowing your energy level, ease of access and ability to maintain the crops will help you determine the ideal type and size of your vegetable garden. Plan the work and then work the plan!

LEFT *This garden is full of scented plants including* Lavandula stoechas *and* Rosa *'Gertrude Jekyll'.*

FRUITS

Depending on where you live, fruit growing can be a satisfying adventure if you choose the appropriate variety for your climate conditions. In some warm and temperate climates several types of fruit will give you a continuous supply during the spring, summer and autumn months. Strawberries can be harvested in the spring, followed by raspberries, blueberries, peaches and apricots during the summer. Grapes ripen in early autumn and then the apple orchards reward us with their bounty.

You can produce many types of fruit in your home garden or retirement community – in the ground, in special pots, trained up a wall and climbing on an arbour. Something that has only recently become an option, thanks to recent research and development in horticulture, is the availability of 'designer' fruit trees that are smaller and more productive. Columnar apple trees serve several roles in the senior's garden – they take up little space and produce great fruit that is very accessible for harvest.

BELOW *Grow climbing vegetables such as green beans for weeks of convenient harvesting and satisfying eating.*

ABOVE *Dwarf fruit trees can produce a plentiful crop of apples that can be harvested easily.*

TREES AND SHRUBS

No garden, however small, should be without its complement of trees or shrubs. They are the bones of any garden: they give scale and contrast to other plants and are a year-round presence when the flowers and vegetables die back. For the senior gardener, choosing these wisely will enhance the garden for many years. Choose trees or shrubs that provide multi-seasonal features, including in the winter months, are tolerant of your particular soil and climate type and require little or no maintenance. Unlike annuals or vegetables that need to be planted each year, a tree or shrub will be permanent, so make sure it is in the right place and give it the recommended care, especially in the first year. (*See also* fruit trees on pages 70–71.)

WILDLIFE

Creating a wildlife habitat in your garden can be one of the most enjoyable by-products of gardening. A healthy garden is one that has a balance of trees and shrubs – both deciduous and evergreen – as well as a diversity of plant material. These leafed and needled plants provide habitat for animals that may want to nest or roost in your garden. Try to include plants that produce nectar, berries, nuts and cones – food for all kinds of animals. Your garden will attract birds and butterflies that will you give you hours of enjoyment and wonder as you watch them in action.

BELOW *Greenfinches enjoy a meal from the feeder as they delight both indoor and outdoor observers.*

WHAT TO PLANT: LOW-MAINTENANCE GARDENS

Besides being familiar with the climatic features of your garden space – sun, shade, wind, soil and moisture – you also need to gauge how much time and energy you are willing or able to commit to your garden. It is sensible to plan your garden as an adaptable feature where the maintenance demands can be changed according to personal preference or your own emerging needs.

ABOVE *Select potted seedlings in preference to sowing seeds to jump-start your spring garden.*

ESTABLISH YOUR MOTIVES

For seniors who spend all their spare time gardening, having a low-maintenance garden might not be a priority. For others who love to garden but also enjoy activities away from home, such as hiking, bird watching and canoeing, finding ways to reduce gardening tasks is highly desirable. If your stamina and strength aren't sufficient to keep up a complex and high-maintenance garden, finding ways to reduce the garden care is a necessity. Finally, some people just want to have more time to sit and relax in their garden rather than working in it. Whatever your situation, here are some options for simplifying your garden space without detracting from its aesthetic appeal.

When making decisions about how to maintain your garden easily you will obviously focus on plants that are 'low-maintenance'. However, you may still choose to grow a few favourite 'difficult' plants, if you are prepared to give extra thought to their care. Here are some of the ongoing maintenance activities that will need to be considered as part of this equation.

EASY PLANTING

The work involved varies depending on the combination of what, where and how much you decide to plant. Making planting easy and accessible probably has as much to do with ensuring ease of access by using raised beds, containers and appropriate positioning in the garden, as with choosing plants that will inspire you to maintain and care for them.

You also need to make sure the seasonal requirements of your choices suit you. Bulbs, for example, need to be put in the ground in most climates in the autumn before the temperatures dip and when you can still work the soil. Similarly, autumn is the best time to plant trees or shrubs, although any time up to late winter is an option, except in very cold areas. For a vegetable garden, late spring or summer is the best time to plant.

Window boxes and containers work on all levels for ease of maintenance. Ensure interest from one season to another by using plants that mature in the early spring, such as lettuces which are cool-weather vegetables, right through to pansies or cyclamen that can be planted in the autumn wherever the winters are milder. Buy seedlings from nurseries and garden supply stores for convenience, or sow and tend your favourite seeds indoors until they are ready for transplanting.

LEFT *A high-rise terrace offers the feel of a garden with its comfortable seating and variety of container plants.*

RIGHT *A patio garden full of rich planting textures can become your outdoor living room for several months in the summer.*

WEEDING

It is advisable to find ways of discouraging weeds because weeding is time-consuming and weeds will affect the health of your plants. By suppressing weeds you will help your soil retain its moisture and nutrients for the 'good' plants, giving you time to do more satisfying things.

You can use chemical or organic herbicides to control weeds. However, avoid using chemicals, as these toxic compounds can affect the flora and fauna in your garden as well as your own health. The exception would be where highly persistent weeds cannot be effectively controlled by hand weeding or mulches.

DEADHEADING

When you deadhead flowers, you channel energy away from the production of seeds and into the creation of more flowers. For many plants, particularly annuals, this garden task promotes repeated flowering on

BELOW *Combine a variety of containers with different heights of plants for an interesting 'garden' on your patio.*

plants that would otherwise stop early on. Deadheading can be done by hand or with scissors or pruners, depending on the nature of the plant. Some senior gardeners will tolerate a garden that loses its bloom early because deadheading does take time and could involve more maintenance than they may want to undertake, but many varieties of plants will perform well without it, so try different ones.

WATERING

A healthy plant is made up of 75 to 90 per cent water, so adequate water is critical during the first few weeks of a plant's growth when the plants are building their root systems and getting established. While well-established plants in the ground can take advantage of the seasonal rains, there will be times when most gardens will need watering. For most gardens the optimal amount of water from rain or watering is two and a half centimetres (an inch) every week, but many established plants could easily tolerate short periods of dryness. If heat and drought are prolonged, then prioritise your most vulnerable plants, especially those that are newly planted.

If you use containers and window boxes, you should assess where they are situated and how this might impede water absorption. If eaves or overhead structures block natural rainfall, then watering will need to be one of your regular garden routines.

LEFT *Ground elder (Aegopodium podagraria 'Variegatum') is a colourful ground cover, but it can be invasive!*

RIGHT *This colourful perennial border hugs and intertwines around the fence and brings dazzling colour to your boundary.*

LOW-MAINTENANCE PLANTS

Unsurprisingly, the plants to choose for a low-maintenance garden are those that don't require a lot of time and fussing. Invariably they won't need staking, which is a big advantage for senior gardeners since this process can be fiddly. A low-maintenance plant will continue to look stunning without frequent deadheading and will also not need frequent dividing or heavy fertilizing.

All growing plants make demands, but these are reduced when you choose the right plants for the local climate and soil conditions, and those that will work with the character of your outdoor space. For example, planting a perennial, evergreen ground cover instead of annual flowers around a tree or in a garden bed will eliminate the annual (and expensive) process of purchase and planting. Plants that suppress weeds, such as bergenia and hosta, or can cope with dry conditions, such as agapanthus and lavender, also have low-maintenance advantages.

DO YOU REALLY WANT A LAWN?

Lawns are a high-maintenance area with yearly schedules of fertilizing, watering and mowing. Another low-maintenance option is to reduce the grass areas in your space by replacing some of it with a thick-growing ground cover such as pachysandra or wild ginger. Other lush and green ground covers will provide the visual impact of a 'green carpet', but need less maintenance than grass requires (*see also* below).

HARD LANDSCAPING

Decks, balconies and front porches can become your low-maintenance garden oases with a few well-chosen plants growing in beautiful and unusual pots. Container gardening can provide you with a way to have a variety of plants and still be able to control their care. Adding a drip system to the pots can even reduce your need to be vigilant about watering. With all the wonderful prepared soil mixtures available you are also free from dealing with poor garden soil.

LEFT *Use less lawn and more low-maintenance plants for a lush garden without all the labour.*

Gaultheria procumbens

Cornus kousa

Coreopsis verticillata

Euonymus alatus 'Fireball'

Sarcococca confusa

LOW-MAINTENANCE OPTIONS

Each plant included in the directory on pages 208–249 has a maintenance categorization, indicating either low, moderate or high care. If you are planning a low-maintenance garden here are some of the least demanding planting options from this selection.

Ground covers

• Wintergreen (*Gaultheria procumbens*) (page 132)
• Allegheny spurge (*Pachysandra procumbens*) (page 134)
• Shuttleworth's ginger (*Asarum shuttleworthii*) (page 128)
• Christmas fern (*Polystichum acrostichoides*) (page 135)

Perennials

• Sedum (*Sedum* 'Herbstfreude') (page 126)
• Moonbeam coreopsis (*Coreopsis verticillata*) (page 123)
• Black-eyed Susan (*Rudbeckia fulgida* var. *sullivantii* 'Goldsturm') (page 126)
• Stella d'oro daylily (*Hemerocallis* 'Stella de Oro') (page 125)
• Purple coneflower (*Echinacea purpurea*) (page 124)

Shrubs

• Abelia (*Abelia* x *grandiflora* 'Little Richard') (page 136)
• Burning bush (*Euonymus alatus* 'Fireball') (page 137)
• Sweet box (*Sarcococca confusa*) (page 141)
• Oak-leaf hydrangea (*Hydrangea quercifolia* 'Snow Queen' or 'Pee Wee') (page 140)

Small trees

• Kousa dogwood (*Cornus kousa*) (page 137)
• Serviceberry (*Amelanchier arborea*) (page 136)
• Crape myrtle (*Lagerstroemia indica*) (page 138)
• Sourwood (*Oxydendron arboreum*) (page 138)

Hydrangea quercifolia

Rudbeckia fulgida var. *sullivantii*

Sedum 'Herbstfreude'

Pachysandra procumbens

Echinacea purpurea

GARDENS TO STIMULATE SIGHT

For most of us, our sense of sight gives us the initial information about a garden. The colours of the flowers, the textures of the leaves and the shapes of the plants all contribute to the picture. The importance of this is unlikely to change, but the sorts of colours and colour combinations that we like may shift as we get older, and any deterioration in our eyesight may require us to change the way our gardens work visually.

ABOVE *Majestic and tall, a bright yellow sunflower will stop people in their tracks as they gaze into the seed-studded disc.*

COLOUR AND CONTRAST

As we age we are likely to have more trouble detecting pale and pastel colours. Having contrasting colours in a garden compensates for this and provides important visual stimuli.

Purple flowers next to yellow, white against green foliage, or orange adjacent to blue will boost the garden experience for ageing eyes. So, to enhance the visual impact in your own garden, plant yellow daffodils

(*Narcissus* spp.) in front of a dark green hedge, or red and orange crocosmia next to white daisies. Both black-eyed Susans (*Rudbeckia fulgida*) and dwarf sunflowers (*Helianthus* spp.) offer this contrast within a single flower.

Vegetables are not just for eating, because they also offer some exciting colours. Consider the humble vegetable Swiss chard (*Beta vulgaris*) that adds a fun splash of colour with the variety 'Bright Lights'. The brightly coloured stems and foliage are as tasty as they are beautiful and look stunning among perennials. Another common vegetable that can serve double duty in your garden is the beetroot (beet) cultivar 'Bull's Blood' (*Beta vulgaris*). This has bright burgundy leaves that are highly attractive in the border.

Matching plants with complementary colours allows you to 'paint' a beautiful garden and these choices will add colour contrast and drama to the garden experience.

CHANGING EYESIGHT

To stay involved in gardening and being outdoors it helps to understand that our eyes adjust more slowly to light levels as we age. They have trouble compensating with abrupt changes in illumination, such as suddenly stepping

LEFT *Red hot pokers (*Kniphofia uvaria*) catch the eye as they stand like brilliant burning candles in front of dark foliage.*

into bright sunlight or entering deep shade. So take care when entering or leaving the garden by sitting a while to get used to the different light levels.

An eye condition such as glaucoma can reduce seniors' ability to distinguish fine details, instead focusing on form and shape. An evergreen tree has a consistent year-round form that orientates the observer well. So we become familiar with the shape of the tall stately fir or the drooping limbs of the weeping cedar.

Mobile elements are another feature that can appeal to those with compromised vision. A gentle breeze means that strands of spiny grasses and tall flowers will catch the wind and start bobbing and weaving.

For those with reduced eyesight, the key to staying active in the garden is learning adaptive techniques that will build competency and confidence.

You can space vegetables or annuals equally in rows using a notched wooden board as your planting template. If you enjoy hand

BELOW *Autumn brings many colours to our attention. Maple trees are especially famous for their brilliant shows.*

ABOVE *A selection of chrysanthemums make a big impact in this bed because of their rich, velvety purple and pinks.*

sowing, use large seeds such as peas, beans and sunflowers, which are easier to handle. Similarly, using seed tapes (accessible from most garden centres) makes planting tiny seeds such as carrots and radishes easy and reliable. Grouping plants with similar watering requirements will help with irrigation tasks. Labels or tags with large lettering or Braille will help you identify special plants or the locations of seeds.

BEAUTIFUL FOLIAGE

When we think of leaves we tend to think of green shades, but foliage can be found in many colours and patterns. A member of the coleus family, for example, will introduce a rainbow of leaf colours into your garden that will mix and match together and with their companions. Another great foliage choice is the chartreuse-coloured ornamental sweet potato, *Solanum tuberosum* 'Margarita'. Finally, caladiums are excellent for those shady or partly shady areas in your garden as they enliven the garden with foliage of

green, white, pink, rose, red and chartreuse. If you can plant them so that the setting sun beams through the leaves, you'll achieve additional visual impact.

MAINTAINING ANNUAL INTEREST

Aim to have a selection of plants that will ensure year-round enjoyment. So you might have green fiddlehead ferns (*Pteridium aquilinum*) that will uncurl in the spring, tomatoes (*Lycopersicon esculentum*) that will ripen deep red on the vines as summer passes, and the opportunity to collect lovely yellow ginkgo (*Ginkgo biloba*) leaves in the autumn. Some seasons will expose structural elements such as interesting branches and colourful bark. A Japanese maple, for example, offers a graceful network of flowing twigs and branches that has considerable presence during its winter dormancy. Winter is also the time that we appreciate how much shape and height contribute to the garden picture.

BELOW *Think contrasting colours when choosing flowers – pair oranges and blues or purples and yellows for a striking effect.*

GARDENS TO STIMULATE SOUND

The ability to hear may deteriorate as we age. However, finding ways of tuning into the sounds in our garden, both naturally occurring ones such as bees collecting pollen and man-made features such as wind chimes, will awaken our auditory sense and enhance our garden experience. With a little practice on our part and the addition of some new features, our gardens can be 'wired' for sound.

ABOVE *Birdfeeders with a variety of seeds will attract many different kinds of birds who will animate your garden with sound.*

RUSTLING GRASSES
Here are a selection of grasses that rustle in the breeze.

- Greater quaking grass (*Briza maxima*)
- Jose select tall wheatgrass (*Elytrigia elongota* 'Jose Select')
- Miscanthus (*Miscanthus sinensis* 'Morning Light') – upright, arching foliage and bronze plumes.
- Miscanthus (*Miscanthus sinensis* 'Silberfeder') – sturdy green foliage and white seed plumes.
- Prairie sky switch grass (*Panicum virgatum* 'Prairie Sky') – tight-growing sky-blue foliage and airy, sand-coloured flower spikes.
- Silver grass (*Miscanthus oligostachyus* 'Nanus Variegatus') – has a pretty bamboo-like foliage.
- Bamboo (*Phyllostachys*) – lovely foliage that appears to whisper in the wind. Their tall and erect stems produce a hollow sound when knocked together.

Panicum virgatum   *Phyllostachys*

RIGHT Briza maxima, *a quaking grass, sounds like a small ripple of water as it catches the wind and quakes in its roots.*

ABOVE *Clinking threaded limpet shells are merely one kind of chime that will add sound and melody to your garden.*

ORIENTATION WITH SOUND
The sounds of nature tell us so much about the habitat in which we are gardening and relaxing. Listening to the low buzz of a bumblebee or the sweet trill from the blackbird will be, quite literally, music to your ears. What's more, sounds in the garden orientate us to what season we are entering or leaving. From the dripping of water droplets from icicles on the eaves to the honking of geese overhead, these simple natural sounds tell us in gentle ways where we are in time.

There are many natural ways to add sounds to your garden. Attracting wildlife such as birds, insects and mammals is one way. Adding plants, such as bamboo, grasses and palms, and flowers that form interesting seed pods can also introduce new auditory

experiences. If you let an area of lawn go unraked in the autumn then you will hear the crunching and crackling of dried leaves underfoot.

Adding man-made features such as wind chimes, bird and squirrel feeders and bird houses will bring many musical and wildlife sounds into your garden. Water channelled through a water feature can create a sense of peace and calm, and have healing benefits. A simple water feature, especially one that flows, bubbles, sprays or drips, will also attract more wildlife. Even if you can only manage a shallow birdbath, you will still enjoy hearing birds splashing about the pool as they flap their wings. For feathered and furry visitors, water features offer a reliable drink and a place to clean themselves.

REDUCING NOISE POLLUTION
Having moving water in the garden can be a creative way to mask offensive sounds such as traffic or machine noise that can disturb the peace. Often referred to as 'white noise', water movement helps drown out traffic and other noise pollution, allowing you to relax undisturbed by the world beyond.

RIGHT *The bright orange pods of the Chinese lantern are an autumn favourite. Plant it in a big pot, as it can be invasive.*

BELOW *Crisp, colourful autumnal leaves carpeting a path will crackle and rustle under your feet.*

PLANTS WITH SEED PODS
Here are some of the seed pods that make attractive sounds:

• Poppies (*Papaver*) have showy blooms, require little care, and form geometric seed pods. Full of seeds for next year's garden, the pods make an attractive rattling sound when shaken.
• The Chinese lantern plant (*Physalis alkekengi*) produces rows of inflated papery, orange-red lantern-like seed pods that can be heard moving in the wind.
• Honesty (*Lunaria annua*) forms disc-like seed pods that change to purple and then brown – rub them to reveal the silver discs that hold the seeds.

• Columbine (*Aquilegia*) is an early summer flowering plant, and one of the easiest perennials. Once the seed heads form and a hint of brown emerges, deadhead them and create a rattle bouquet from the pods.
• Love-in-a-mist (*Nigella damascena*) is a delicate plant, showy in the spring with bright blue, white or rose-coloured flowers, but the fun starts when it forms paper-textured puffy seed heads which rattle when shaken. The minute black seeds will ensure next year's growth.
• The money plant (*Lunaria biennis*) has lightly scented purple or white flowers in the spring and translucent, silver-dollar seed pods that flutter gently in the wind.

Nigella damascena   *Lunaria annua*   *Aquilegia*   *Papaver*

GARDENS TO STIMULATE SMELL

Our sense of smell brings alive our experience of gardens. The perfume of a rose can capture a special memory, and the garden after rainfall is filled with the aroma of moist earth and greenery. However, this sense does deteriorate as we age. It might also be compromised by certain medications or being a smoker. Whatever our nasal ability, there are plants – and not just flowers – that are sure to stimulate and delight.

ABOVE *The sweet fragrances of old-fashioned climbing roses fill the air and say, "Come in for a closer look".*

SEASONAL PERFUMES

Fragrances can elevate our mood and increase our feelings of well-being and overall happiness. Whether from sweet-smelling blooms, pungent leaves or strong herbal essences, olfactory stimulation is undoubtedly one of the joys of gardening.

Each season brings its own unique scents that can remind us of our past history in gardens. Even if you are tending just a large container, you can still grow fragrant plants.

In the springtime, sweet-smelling shrubs sited near your entranceway will welcome visitors to your garden. Low-maintenance daphnes, lilacs (*Syringa* spp.) and many deciduous azaleas can dazzle you and your visitors with their charming perfumes. Think about the subtle scents created by spring bloomers such as violets (*Viola* spp.), lily of the valley (*Convallaria majalis*), stocks (*Malcolmia maritima*), pinks (*Dianthus* spp.) and sweet alyssum (*Lobularia maritima*). Summertime mock oranges (*Philadelphus coronarius*) and roses (*Rosa* spp.) will stop you in your tracks as you are greeted by their wafting aromas. In the autumn, flowers on Chinese holly (*Osmarea* x *burkwoodii*) or osmanthus offer fabulously sweet smells.

In the winter, sweet box (*Sarcococca*) packs such a scent in its tiny, inconspicuous flowers that people have been known to think that someone has been using too much perfume. This can be uplifting for those of us who can feel down in the short, dark days of winter.

LEFT *Plants including mountain pine (*Pinus mugo*), lavender (*Lavandula stoechas*), *Rosa* 'Gertrude Jekyll', bronze fennel (*Foeniculum vulgare purpureum*) and iris create an experience that will linger all day.*

WHERE TO SITE SCENTED PLANTS AND SHRUBS

Planting fragrant plants near the entrance to your garden will perfume the area as you enter. Another idea is to add plants with aromatic leaves to places with a narrow span where you will be brushing against the plant, for example as you walk under an archway. Scents are stronger and easier to detect when the sun is shining and the temperature is warm, so an arbour covered with honeysuckle or fragrant clematis needs only a sunny day to create a perfumed experience. Sweet peas trained on wires against a sunny wall will also create sweet aromas.

If you don't have room for scented shrubs, then create a fragrant container or raised bed with various scented geraniums (*Pelargonium* spp.). These come in perfumes that include apple, lime, nutmeg, pine, lemon and rose. They are powerhouses of fragrance and bloom all through the summer and into the autumn.

USING HERBS

Herbs are great way to keep fragrances alive in a garden space, whether they are planted at ground level, in a raised

BELOW *A path under a covered archway of blooming sweet peas may be one of the sweetest walks you ever take.*

bed or in a container. Planting some scented thymes (*Thymus subphylum*) and other herbs between pavers or stones offers an effortless way to activate fragrance. Walking on them will crush the leaves, causing them to emit their aroma into the air.

Familiar favourites, such as rosemary, lavender and mint, will provide you with months of classic scents that might motivate you to use them in other ways – for teas, seasoning or crafts. Or, if you're feeling more adventurous, try unfamiliar herbs such as the curry plant (*Helichrysum italicum*). In addition to having a heightened aroma – on sunny days its yellow flowers fill the air with a spicy fragrance – this evergreen plant has other attractive features. The foliage is a variegated silver-grey in colour and has a wonderfully attractive fuzzy texture.

ABOVE *Fragrant thyme is a great herb to grow among walking pavers where it is hot and dry. A slight foot pressure will release the thyme's lovely aroma.*

BELOW *Grow lily of the valley (*Convallaria majalis*) in a pot and site it in an area where you can benefit from its perfume.*

GARDENS TO STIMULATE TOUCH

Unlike the other senses, the sense of touch seems to be retained no matter what our age. Certainly, few things are more satisfying for gardeners than digging their fingers into the soft earth. Reassuringly, the sense of touch is always there to fall back on, providing a way of connecting with the world around us if other senses are less reliable. Here we look at the possibilities for stimulating this grounding sense in the garden.

ABOVE Sempervivum tectorum *has sculpted leaf forms, tight rosettes that appear waxed and polished.*

SMOOTH AND SOFT TEXTURES

Adding smooth and soft textures to your garden can have a calming effect. Good examples are lamb's ear (*Stachys byzantina*), with its velvety long leaves, and springtime pussy willows (*Salix caprea*) with its soft, grey bundles.

WAXY AND LEATHERY TEXTURES

Plants that grow in the desert often have a waxy, waterproof coating, such as the Christmas cactus (*Schlumbergera* spp.), or *Bergenia cordifolia*, whose leathery leaves squeak when rubbed together!

ROUGH AND SPIKY TEXTURES

Many tree barks feel rough and have highly textured nooks and crannies for curious fingers to explore. Alternatively, the stems and foliage of the purple coneflower (*Echinacea purpurea*) have stiff hairs that give them a rasping, sandpapery quality.

PAPERY TEXTURES

Some flowers provide interesting seed pods, such as the money plant (*Lunaria biennis*) with its papery layers. Pearly everlasting (*Anaphalis margaritacea*) produces white, papery bracts with flowers in tight clusters at the top of the stem. When moved, they sound just like paper rustling.

OTHER DELIGHTS

Digging our toes into lush, cool grass can refresh and relax us. A small water feature with a place to cool your feet would be an excellent addition to a sensory garden. Adding aquatic plants, such as water lilies, water lettuce, water grasses and bulrushes will provide other interesting tactile experiences.

BELOW *The Himalayan cherry (*Prunus rufa*) has attractive peeling, reddish-brown bark.*

BELOW Scirpus *grass produces small fluffy flowers at the stem tips.*

BELOW *The Chinese snowball (*Viburnum macrocephalum*) forms soft flower clusters.*

GARDENS TO STIMULATE TASTE

Admiring the colourful produce in a vegetable or fruit garden is a small step away from knowing how the ripe green cucumber or the plump red strawberries taste. Other garden elements to enliven our taste buds might be a bed of edible flowers, a container of herbs or a vine of sweet honeysuckle. Because the sense of taste becomes less acute as we age, let's take measures in our gardens to keep it alive and well.

ABOVE *Harvesting fruit that you have grown is one of the most satisfying experiences for a gardener.*

ABOVE *Many flowers are edible and good for you – add nasturtium flowers to your salads for colour and a peppery taste.*

ABOVE *Growing fruit and vegetables that you can eat in the garden provides the perfect, healthy afternoon nibble.*

THE VEGETABLE GARDEN

There is nothing more rewarding than harvesting sweet cherry tomatoes from pots in your patio. Other delicious vegetables you can grow include greens, such as spring greens (collards) and kale (*Brassica oleracea* var. *acephala*), mustard greens (*Brassica* spp.), rocket (arugula), chard (*Beta vulgaris* subsp. *cicla*) and lettuce (*Lactuca sativa*), with tasty leaves full of vitamins and antioxidants. There are also pole or bush beans, one of the most reliable and tasty crops to grow.

Potatoes (*Solanum tuberosum*) can be cultivated in a 45-litre (12-gallon) bucket or raised bed. These are easy to plant, maintain, and harvest. Small, fingerling types taste especially buttery.

Squash (*Cucurbita pepo*) is another option – there are summer and winter varieties. Cucumbers (*Cucumis sativus*) can be grown on a trellis to save space.

FRUIT CROPS

The possibilities for fruit growing are extensive. If you do not have room for full-sized apple trees, use small columnar or dwarf ones, ideally two or three to ensure pollination. Grapes can be grown almost anywhere, and selected varieties in warm areas will ripen over a long season.

Strawberries are a must-have for a small garden, so find a variety that will do well in your conditions. Blueberries are a small shrub that can serve as both an ornamental plant and a fruit bearer.

HERBAL TASTES

Flavouring food with fresh herbs makes cooking and eating a more exciting experience. The ideal time for picking them is in the morning before the sun gets hot and the leaves wilt. Store them in an open bag or perforated plastic bag in your refrigerator and they will last for several days.

Many herbal flowers and leaves make lovely teas. These include lemon verbena (*Aloysia triphylla*), raspberry and blackberry leaves, and hibiscus flowers.

EDIBLE FLOWERS

Herbs and some plants produce flowers that can be eaten. Nasturtiums, marigolds (*Calendula officinalis*), roses (*Rosa*), scented geraniums (*Pelargonium*) and dandelions (*Taraxacum officinale*) are all easy to grow. If you like spicy and savoury flavours, use fresh nasturtiums, young dandelions or marigold petals in salads or sprinkled on the top of rice. Rose and carnation petals are sweet and attractive additions to desserts. Scented geranium flowers offer many flavours, including citrus. Sprinkle the blossoms over desserts, add them to cool drinks or freeze them in ice cubes as a floating garnish.

Light purple chive blooms can be tossed on salads to add an onion scent and flavour, and lavender flowers can be added to cookies. Sweet basil flowers sprinkled over a salad or pasta add strong flavour and a spark of colour. Yellow dill flowers are a great seasoning for soups, seafood and salad dressings.

FLOWER AND HERB GARDENS

If you have pre-selected flowers and herbs as components of your age-proof garden, the next stage is to visualize them. Would you like a luxurious bed of roses; a space for spring flowers such as daffodils and grape hyacinths; fragrant clematis and sweet peas to hide an unsightly wall; or perhaps a kitchen garden with fresh herbs?

For flower gardens, we look at the different types of flowers – annuals, perennials, biennials and bulb – with an emphasis on perennials because they come back year after year and require less work. There is also a delightful illustration of a border for lasting colour to give you planting ideas, and a project showing how to plant and stake dahlia tubers.

For herb gardens, we consider useful herbs for cooking, such as parsley and rosemary, and also their visual impact and the colours and scents that characterize them. There is a colour plan of a herb circle to delight the senses with 14 featured herbs, including yarrow, camomile and meadowsweet. Finally, we look at the practicalities of planting a herb container, including choosing the right soil to give its contents the very best start.

OPPOSITE *A small patio garden can be made more welcoming with flowering vines, containers and climbing roses.*

ABOVE *Wooden raised beds give easy-to-access gardens for your flowers, herbs and vegetables.*

ABOVE Doronicum orientale *is a tough herbaceous plant that will bring sunshine to your borders in return for very little effort.*

ABOVE *Small pots of assorted herbs growing on a garden table – creating a colourful corner that is also easy to access.*

FLOWER GARDENS

Flower gardens are like quilts – true labours of love. Although one may have the same colours, shapes and sizes as another, it's the creativity, vision and craftsmanship of the quilter that makes each different and unique. So it is with gardens, but particularly with flower gardens. The colours, shapes, sizes and textures of the flowers we use to create our own unique garden are the elements that make each space different, special and personal.

ABOVE *Radiant blooms of bold colours such as this poppy add interesting textures to your flower garden.*

PLANNING A FLOWER GARDEN

Earlier in the book we discovered how the practical aspects of our garden space influence our decisions about what to grow. We shouldn't, however, underestimate the aesthetic or sentimental aspects of why we choose certain plants. Flowers such as tall pink hollyhocks or fragrant climbing yellow roses may ground our selections, evoking memories of the gardens we grew up in, where we learned to sow and observe the flowers that have played a role in our lives.

MIXED FLOWER GARDENS

For some older gardeners, keeping up a complex flower garden can be a challenge. While we may still yearn to have flowers around us, our enthusiasm

ABOVE *Petunias are familiar perennials that will fill a container with vibrant, season-long colour and shape.*

for their care may wane as we come to terms with limitations of space, energy and mobility. Other senior gardeners may be motivated to maintain a variety of flowerbeds. If your resources allow, it is rewarding to have a colourful mix of perennials, annuals, climbers, biennials, bulbs and ground covers with variations in height and foliage texture.

In larger spaces, flower gardens can be punctuated with small evergreen shrubs or small deciduous trees to give interest when flowering ceases. Annuals, perennials, biennials and flowers grown from bulbs are described in more detail below and overleaf.

Another idea is to grow a three- or four-season garden that has something in flower at every stage of the year – snowdrops and hellebores during the winter; brightly coloured daffodils (*Narcissus*) and tulips throughout the spring; daisies, geraniums and catmint (*Nepeta*) in the summer; and dahlias and chrysanthemums in the autumn.

ANNUALS

Plants that complete their life cycles in one year or less are described as annuals. In this time they germinate, grow shoots and leaves, produce flowers, set seeds and then die. Many tender perennials are treated as annuals in temperate climates, as they are killed by frost, so new plants need to be bought or sown indoors for next year's garden. Examples of annuals are morning glory (*Ipomoea purpurea*), French marigolds

(*Tagetes signata pumila*), and species such as *Impatiens*, *Tropaeolum* (nasturtium), *Zinnia, Nicotiana, Petunia* and *Verbena*. In temperate climates, hardy annuals with more frost tolerance may return the following year, good examples being pot marigolds (*Calendula officinalis*), cornflower (*Centaurea cyanus*), larkspur (*Consolida* spp.), sweet alyssum (*Lobularia maritima*) and Virginia stocks (*Malcolmia maritima*). There are many different kinds of annuals that are reliable bloomers from spring until autumn. They not only provide colour to the garden, but are great for bouquets and flower pressing.

OPPOSITE *Roses climbing on a picket fence adorn a garden, but remember that "Every rose has its thorns".*

ABOVE *Marigolds and Californian poppies (*Eschscholzia californica*) are colourful, versatile plants that liven up a large space.*

PERENNIALS

Flowers that have a perennial habit live for at least two years, and many endure for years. This type of flower reduces our need to buy and replant each season. Most perennials bloom in only one, or at the most two seasons during the year. Because perennials typically bloom in spring, summer or autumn, you should situate them in your garden where you can enjoy them when they are in season.

Even when perennials are not flowering, many of them offer interesting foliage and stem structures that can extend their visual appeal. Coreopsis, coneflowers (*Echinacea*), black-eyed Susan (*Rudbeckia fulgida*), daisies (*Bellis perennis*), columbines (*Aquilegia*) and catmint (*Nepeta*) are a small sampling of rewarding perennials to include in a flower garden. Because it is generally true that perennials are less labour-intensive than other options, these are likely to appeal to gardeners with less time and energy and are explored in more detail on pages 46–47.

BIENNIALS

Flowers that are biennial typically complete their life cycle in two years. In their first year they grow from seed and form leaves and roots but no flowers. They survive winter and then burst into blossom the following year before they set seed and die. Common biennials to have in your garden include sweet William (*Dianthus barbatus*), foxgloves (*Digitalis purpurea*) and hollyhocks (*Alcea rosea*).

BULBS

Generally classed as bulbs are all those plants that die down to the ground every year and survive as an underground storage organ formed from a modified stem, bud or root:

ABOVE *A stone trough contains flowering spring bulbs such as Daffodils (*Narcissus *'Tête-à-tête'), Chinese Sacred Lily (*Narcissus tazetta*) and low-growing primroses.*

bulbs, corms, rhizomes and tubers. Most of these will flower for many years, often multiplying naturally. Anemones, irises, hyacinths, dahlias, crocus, tulips (*Tulipa*) and daffodils (*Narcissus*) are popular examples of this flower category.

BULBS FOR BORDERS

Planting informal groups of the same bulb can be highly effective and, depending on the size of the border, the groups may be repeated a number of times, with bedding plants or other herbaceous perennials between them. A bed of tulips may be surrounded by forget-me-nots (*Myosotis*) or pansies (*Viola*). Groups of allium may be grown through nearby wallflowers (*Erysimum cheiri*), while gladioli might appear behind penstemons or earlier flowering poppies (*Papaver*).

Lilies are hardy bulbs and can be planted in autumn or late winter. However, they dislike sitting in wet ground, much preferring well-drained soil. If your soil is naturally heavy, add a generous layer of grit in the bottom of the hole as you plant lily bulbs.

LEFT *Well-planned perennial flowerbeds will reliably give continuous seasonal colour, shape and texture.*

Design focus: a flower border for lasting colour

A flower garden is a space with a mixture of flowering plants chosen for their colourful blossoms, interesting foliage and structure. This illustration offers you a guide for planting a simple, yet animated flower border that combines annuals and perennials. Stable stepping stones are placed among the plants so that access to the border is easy. With planning and imagination your flower border can be an exciting combination of colour, height, texture and extended blooming time.

Early in the summer, the yellow 'Stella de Oro' daylilies will produce an abundance of big, showy flowers. The red zinnias, orange-red *Crocosmia* 'Lucifer', and the ever-popular black-eyed Susan were chosen for their mid-season and late blooms. The warm hues of the colour wheel are used – reds, oranges and yellows – and then, for a bit of contrast, some purple flowers and foliage are added.

When you create your design, think about the mature heights of each plant to provide enough room for growth without overpowering other plants. For example, the 'Stella de Oro' daylilies are shorter than most daylilies, so place them in front of taller plants. Forming a floral border with white sweet alyssum defines the garden edge and gives long-lasting fragrant flowers that attract pollinators.

PLANTING LIST

1. Montbretia (*Crocosmia* 'Lucifer')
2. Black-eyed Susan (*Rudbeckia fulgida*)
3. Purple aster (*Aster* x *frikartii* 'Mönch') (*see* picture above)
4. Purple sage (*Salvia officinalis*)
5. Pink petunia (*Petunia* x *hybrida*)
6. Daylily (*Hemerocallis* 'Stella de Oro')
7. White alyssum (*Lobularia maritima*)
8. Red dwarf zinnia (*Zinnia* spp.)

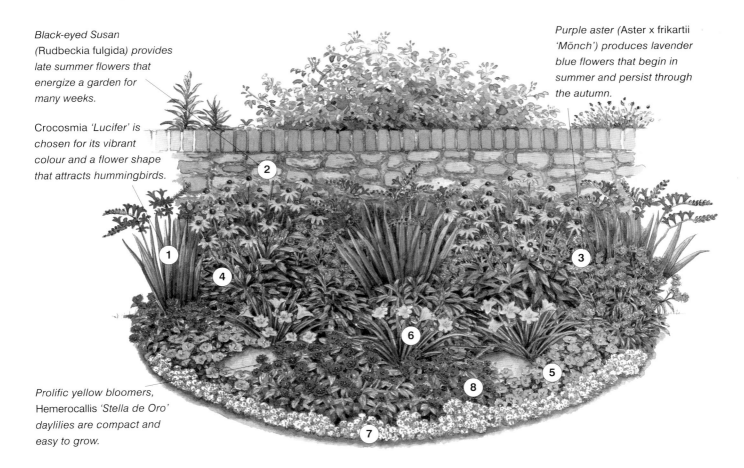

*Black-eyed Susan (*Rudbeckia fulgida*) provides late summer flowers that energize a garden for many weeks.*

Crocosmia 'Lucifer' is chosen for its vibrant colour and a flower shape that attracts hummingbirds.

*Purple aster (*Aster* x frikartii 'Mönch') produces lavender blue flowers that begin in summer and persist through the autumn.*

Prolific yellow bloomers, Hemerocallis 'Stella de Oro' daylilies are compact and easy to grow.

LEFT Sedum spectabile *is a lush succulent with blue-green leaves and dome-shaped pinkish flowers that appear in the autumn.*

RIGHT *Rose bay willow herb (*Epilobium angustifolium*) is a handsome wild flower that will bloom for about a month. Some dismiss it as an invasive weed, others adore its wild character.*

EASY-CARE PERENNIALS

A perennial flowerbed is an ornamental garden that continues to bloom and grow year after year without the need to replant and spend money on new flowers. This is a popular, low-maintenance choice for senior gardeners. While perennial plants tend to be more expensive than annuals (though some are easy to grow from seed), in the long run your investment pays off in reducing both your labour and the need to replace plants regularly.

Many gardeners like to add new things to a perennial bed each year – colourful annuals, bulbs or even decorative vegetables – to accent the garden during low-bloom periods, but a well-designed perennial garden can stand on its own.

If you would like to concentrate on perennials, research those that do well in your area. You should also assess your garden in terms of its sun and shade conditions and select perennial varieties that will thrive in your microclimate. For example, creating a perennial garden in a shady area will require plants that may not have the most colourful and showiest of blooms, but will allow you to showcase an amazing collection of foliage. If you have a garden in desert-style conditions or in a very sunny and dry area, for example, consider plants from the often-overlooked sedum family, which have a vast array of shapes, sizes and colours.

Perennial colour and texture

Deciding on the colours you want can be one of the most enjoyable aspects of flower gardening. Colour has a great influence on the mood of a perennial garden – cool, pastel shades create tranquillity and calmness while the hot colours inject a feeling of excitement and energy. All the shades of green – usually the colour of the leaves – form the neutral portion of the palette. When making your selections keep in mind that our sensibility to certain colours, especially blue, diminishes as we age, whereas our preferences for other colours such as green and red increase.

LEFT *A thoughtful perennial border starts with spring bloomers, features interesting foliage and uses colours that balance and harmonize.*

ABOVE *Mixing a variety of blossoms makes an interesting collage of flower shapes that will attract pollinators.*

One strategy to give a bold colour punch to the garden is to choose complementary shades of blue, orange and yellow perennials. Alternatively, you can stay within one section of the colour wheel to create a calming perennial garden with floral shades of pinks and lavenders and subtle sage greens for the foliage.

Texture and form always add interest, so look for plants that have unique structures such as Jerusalem sage (*Phlomis fruticosa*), ornamental grasses, and the Hinoki false cypress (*Chamaecyparis*). These all enhance the personality of the garden by giving it unusual form and airiness.

When perennials are in full bloom the form, structure or foliage is less noticeable, but for 80 per cent of the time all that we see is foliage. So choose plants that have broad, shapely leaves, such as hostas, or the smaller foliage of astilbe, with dazzling green leaves that turn to a mixture of burgundy and purple. Tall spiky ferns can also be attractive.

Controlling perennial choices

Because there are so many varieties of plants available from all over the world, the vast choice can be overwhelming, and it is tempting to pack in as many different flowers as you can. Many gardeners love the chaotic, exuberant effect this creates, while others prefer a simpler design, which can be equally striking if carefully thought out. This is a matter of personal taste, but remember that more varieties will usually mean more maintenance.

Another approach is to create a perennial theme garden. For example, you might choose a fragrant garden with roses, lavender, phlox, stock and dianthus creating layers of scent and pretty blossoms in a sunny area. Alternatively, you could create a butterfly garden that might include plants that are rich in nectar, such as nepeta, salvia, scabiosa, Indian blanket flower (*Gaillardia* spp.) and bergamot (*Monarda*). Butterflies also appreciate flowers that have flat tops like Queen Anne's lace (*Daucus carota*), parsley flowers (*Petroselinum*) and yarrow (*Achillea millefolium*) so they can easily land in the garden, rest on the flat surfaces and absorb the warm sun.

RELIABLE PERENNIAL PLANTS: A STARTER PACK

Galium odoratum   *Campanula*

Small trees and shrubs
- Rose of Sharon (*Hibiscus calycinum*)
- Box (*Buxus sempervirens*)
- Hinoki cypress (dwarf variety) (*Chamaecyparis obtusa* 'Nana Aurea')
- Dwarf rhododendron (*Rhododendron* spp.)
- Dwarf hydrangeas (*Hydrangea* spp.)

Tall perennials
- Shasta daisies (*Leucanthemum superbum*)
- Phlox (*Phlox paniculata* 'Franz Schubert')
- Joe Pye weed (*Eupatorium maculatum*)
- Giant fleece flower (*Persicaria polymorpha*)
- Ornamental grasses
- Asters (*Aster* spp.)
- Sneezeweed (*Helenium autumnale* 'Butterpat')

Intermediate-size perennials
- Tickseed (*Coreopsis*)
- Bellflower (*Campanula*)
- Salvia (*Salvia splendens*)
- Gypsyweed (*Veronica officinalis*)
- Heuchera (*Heuchera* spp.)
- Daylily (*Hemerocallis* spp.)
- Gay feather (*Liatris spicata*)

Low-growing perennials
- Alyssum (*Lobularia* spp.)
- Sweet woodruff (*Galium odoratum*)
- Golden-edged thyme (*Thymus vulgaris* 'Aureus')
- Silver brocade artemisia (*Artemisia* 'Silver Brocade')
- Sand strawberry (*Fragaria chiloensis*)

Project: planting and prestaking dahlia tubers

Planting dahlias as soon as the ground is warm to about 15°C (60°F) will give you flower colour all summer long and into the autumn. By choosing healthy tubers, siting them in a very sunny spot (at least 8 hours each day) and preparing the ground, you'll have these quick growers as constant companions in your flower garden. Once you can stake them to support their growth, dahlias are easy to manage and bring colourful rewards.

ABOVE *Dahlia blossoms come in many shapes, sizes and colours and are worth the care required to get them started.*

MATERIALS
- Healthy, firm tubers that are large and free of nicks, cuts or signs of rot
- Equal mix of humus, compost, sharp sand and well-rotted manure
- Shovel
- Stakes
- Soft twine

GARDENER'S NOTE
At step 3, the hole should remain partially filled with just the top of the stem sticking up until you begin to see growth. (Do not add fertilizer or water at this time; wait until you see green shoots appear.)

1 *Dig a planting hole at least twice as deep as the length of the dahlia tuber – and equally as wide. Reserve the soil you removed and add a few shovels of the amendment mix.*

2 *For the taller dahlia varieties, drive a sturdy stake near the planting hole before planting. This ensures that the tuber will not be pierced later in the season when staking is necessary.*

3 *Place the tuber horizontally in the bottom of the hole with the eye pointing upwards. Cover with soil to the top of the stem.*

4 *As the plant grows, gradually add soil to fill the hole and feed every 3 weeks with a balanced fertilizer.*

5 *With the taller and the larger-headed dahlias, tie twine around the stem and then to the stake to offer support.*

HERB GARDENS

From ancient times people have been growing and tending herb gardens. The earliest herb gardens, called 'apothecary gardens', were cultivated for medicinal reasons. Some herbs were used to dye fabric. Some of the medicinal herbs, such as mint and camomile, were also used simply to make a refreshing alternative to tea. Nowadays our main use for herbs is to flavour food and drinks, but many herbs, and therefore herb gardens, are also attractive and pleasantly scented.

ABOVE *Muted colours of purple and golden sage create a lovely and accessible back-door container.*

HERBS FOR THE KITCHEN

As we age, we are encouraged to reduce our intake of salt. Using herbs from the garden as taste enhancers can help us cut down on salt without losing the character of the flavours. Sometimes, too, as we get older, our taste buds need more of a boost to detect flavour. Using fresh or dried herbs from our gardens can enhance foods so that we continue to get enjoyment from eating well-seasoned healthy meals.

Whether you're still gardening in your family home, in a new patio garden or in containers, locate your herb garden so you have easy access.

If you place a culinary herb garden in a handy spot, you'll be more likely to use and enjoy your herbs daily. In the garden bed, put the taller plants, like fennel and rosemary, towards the back. Because you'll want easy access to the herbs, place stepping-stones or pavers in the bed so that you can walk safely and easily up to all the plants.

CREATING IMPACT

If you like designing with colours and textures and are not so focused on growing edible herbs, you'll enjoy the creative aspect of making a herb garden. The muted grey and silver foliage of some types of sage (*Salvia officinalis*), lavender (*Lavandula* spp.), silver thyme (*Thymus vulgaris*) and wormwood (*Artemisia absinthium*) inspire herb gardeners to create a quiet and soothing day garden that will also shimmer as a night garden in the moonlight.

A popular approach is to enjoy a combination of edible herbs with other garden plants and shrubs. Used in this way, herbs not only give the garden a rich palette of colour, texture and usefulness, but attract beneficial insects and important pollinators to breathe new life into our gardens. Parsley plants tucked in among annuals will fill a spot with luxuriant, textured green foliage that will outlast many flowers. Sweet woodruff (*Galium odoratum*) and camomile (*Anthemis nobilis*) will embrace the edges of a perennial bed with their sweet scents. A carpet of chives around the base of your favourite roses may help reduce fungal diseases. In short, herbs are low-maintenance plants that are beautiful, edible, and are beneficial companions to other plants. What more could a gardener want?

LEFT *Herbs can be tightly tucked in a sunny corner of the garden or as border plants for a path.*

OPPOSITE *A cosy crowd of herbs is happy growing together in their wattle raised beds, creating an old-worldly feel.*

EASY HERB CHOICES

Most herbs are easy to grow given the right growing conditions. From an enormous selection of undemanding options, a first-time herb grower might choose examples such as mint, dill, parsley, fennel, chives, thyme, sweet marjoram, sage, rosemary and rocket (arugula). The choice is great, so there is always something to offer a gardener with only a small garden space.

WHERE TO GROW HERBS

Herbs can be grown in a range of settings, such as custom-designed herb gardens and ornamental borders. They can also be grown as companion plants in the vegetable garden and are eminently suited to growing in containers, hanging baskets and window boxes. They are especially useful if grown near the kitchen, so make sure you have practical and easy access.

Herbs range from tall showy herbaceous plants such as fennel (*Foeniculum vulgare*) and tansy (*Tanacetum vulgare*) to ground-hugging cushion plants such as thyme (*Thymus*

ABOVE *Restrict the spread of invasive plants such as mint by planting them in bottomless pots within the ground.*

vulgaris). The majority of herbs originate from dry sunny environments and so need sunshine to help them develop their essential oils. It is best to site herbs in an open, sunny spot in the garden where they will thrive.

Some herbs may be too easy to grow and prone to spread fast, such as peppermint, spearmint and lemon balm. For this reason, all mints are best grown either in containers, or using the traditional method of sinking a large bottomless pot or bucket in the ground and planting them in that.

ABOVE *Hardscapes such as walls and steps offer distinctive spaces in which to display the many textures and varieties of potted herbs.*

SOIL PREPARATION

Drier sites suit most herbs, and the sunnier and hotter the site the better they will taste. The taste and smell of herbs is usually due to the production of essential oils within the plants. If grown in hot conditions, then the concentrations of essential oils will be greater. Growing herbs in very moist rich soils can accelerate their growth, but will result in a milder flavour. They will also look better and flower less than their 'hot-site' counterparts and be easier to harvest.

Herbs are, however, best grown in a soil that is loamy with some added organic matter. The ideal pH is 6.5 to 7.0.

Herbs may be sown directly in the soil outdoors, just like vegetables, which prefer the same soil pH range. The preparation of the seedbed and the sowing techniques are the same, so herbs can easily be interplanted or block planted among vegetables.

LEFT *A basket-woven rustic hurdle fence keeps a burgeoning garden of mixed herbs in place on this patio.*

Allium sativum

Foeniculum vulgare

Ocimum basilicum

Salvia officinalis 'Purpurascens'

Origanum vulgare

Petroselinum neapolitanum

Rosmarinus officinalis

Salvia officinalis

ITALIAN HERBS FOR YOUR GARDEN

If you plan to use herbs for cooking, select those that deliver your favourite flavours. Lovers of Italian food will most likely want herbs such as basil, oregano, and sage in their herb garden. Mint, saffron and coriander (cilantro) will be important if Middle Eastern cuisine is to your liking. Choosing herbs that complement your cooking will make your choices easy and fun.

A fun way to start is to create a themed garden, such as an Italian selection of herbs. Listed below and illustrated above are some basic herbs you will find in many Italian food recipes. *Mangia tutto*!

Allium sativum (garlic) is unique in that it grows from a bulb and is planted in autumn in temperate climates but in spring in cold areas. These hardy plants will emerge in the spring, so when the leaves turn brown, you can harvest the plump, firm cloves.

Foeniculum vulgare (fennel) is popular because the leaves and the seeds can be used for cooking – the leaves for flavouring salads and sauces, and the seeds for bringing out the flavour that makes Italian sausage so delicious. Harvest the greens when still young, since the plant loses its flavour as it ages. Let a few plants mature and go to seed so that you can harvest these.

Ocimum basilicum (basil) is a tender annual herb that is easy to grow provided you put it in very free-draining soil in a warm, sunny position, sheltered from cold winds. Next to your peppers or tomatoes, basil is said to improve their flavour and keeps away flies and mosquitoes!

Origanum vulgare (oregano) is decorative as well as delicious. At maturity, it sprouts lovely little purple flowers, which are edible. The leaves are used fresh from the plant or dried. Oregano is one of the few herbs that, when dried, has a stronger flavour. It should not be harvested until it has flowered, since the flavour is then at its fullest. Because oregano is a vigorous grower, you may want this in a separate, but nearby container.

Petroselinum neapolitanum (Italian parsley) is sweeter than the curly leaf type and is much more flavourful. The leaves are flat and broad, so the chopping is easier. This is an easy herb to grow in full or partial sunlight. This plant is attractive to bees, butterflies and birds. Use it to garnish vegetables, meats and soups – it will enhance the taste of a wide range of dishes.

Rosmarinus officinalis (rosemary) is a fragrant herb that can grow into a small shrub or can cascade over the side of a container. Pick the form you like to combine with the other Italian herbs, and give it full sun. Rosemary is used extensively in lamb and chicken dishes as well as in breads.

Salvia officinalis (sage), like oregano, is both edible and decorative, with delightful leaf colours and variegations. You can harvest the leaves at any time, but they are at their best just before or just after blooming. The grey leaf variety is the best for cooking but should always be used sparingly as it can be overpowering.

PRUNING LAVENDER

Lavender plants are very easy to manage if you get a pruning routine established. A first-year plant will require little or no pruning, since it produces very few flower stalks. Thereafter you should prune hardy lavenders at the end of the summer just as the flowers fade, so they have time to put on a little growth and overwinter as neat, sturdy bushes.

1 *Time the pruning of your lavender bushes to coincide with the end of the flowering period when all that remains is straggly stems.*

2 *Using secateurs (pruners), cut the foliage back to 23cm (9in) or to a point where you can still see green shoots. Don't cut into the old wood: it will not resprout.*

3 *Regular pruning will keep lavender plants in good shape and should ensure that the bush does not become woody in the centre.*

PLANTING YOUR HERB GARDEN

Herbs can be sited anywhere as long as it is sunny. They often make valuable additions to the ornamental garden. Foxgloves (*Digitalis*), sage (*Salvia officinalis*) and the curry plant (*Helichrysum italicum*) are a few examples that can be used in annual and herbaceous borders as well as in the kitchen garden. Remember to contain invasive herbs such as mint in a pot when growing them among other plants in an ornamental border. Remove the flower-heads from the mint before they have had a chance to seed, as the seed will germinate all over your border.

Because herbs need to be pruned often to encourage fresh, leafy growth, cut off the flowers so that they continue to flourish. When plants flower, it is a sign for them to make seeds and eventually die. Unless they are purely to enhance your garden, be vigilant with flowering herbs such as oregano and basil. Hard as it might be, cut off the flowers as soon as you see them and you will increase your harvest of succulent and tasty herbal leaves throughout the season.

POT-PLANTED HERBS

Herbs make excellent subjects for pots and are wonderful for patio gardens that catch plenty of summer sun, although you need to make sure that the potting mix never dries out. Raised beds, which provide good drainage, are also good areas for growing herbs. Always plant them in a free-draining potting mix that won't become waterlogged.

LEFT *Mix herbs among your vegetables or flowers to create an interesting tapestry of plants and to protect against pests.*

Design focus: a herb circle to delight the senses

This garden plan shows a herb circle, a traditional format for a herb garden originating from the sacred medicine wheels used by the Native Americans, the wheel representing the circle of life and the changing seasons. You may not have the space or inclination to do a whole wheel, but you could design a smaller one, or consider replicating a part of it. Using aromatic herbs, such as lavender, sage and thyme, will create magical aromas with the power to stop gardeners in their tracks.

This herb wheel would have to be sited in a warm, sunny spot as herbs thrive in direct sun. Many herbs have subtle colours and interesting foliage and these can be used, as here, to mix hues and textures in compelling combinations.

Growing the aromatic creeping thyme on the edge of a path or in small cracks between paving stones, where they will be stepped on, will activate the scents of the essential oils. Stepping stones have also been placed near the planting to ensure easy access.

Herbs attract various beneficial insects that prey on garden pests. Having a water receptacle, such as a bird bath, near your herbs will hydrate the butterflies that will visit.

PLANTING LIST

1 Purple coneflower (*Echinacea purpurea*)
2 Purple sage (*Salvia officianalis* 'Purpurea')
3 Rosemary (*Rosmarinus officinalis*)
4 Flowering onion (*Allium atropurpureum*)
5 Creeping thyme (*Thymus praecox* 'Albiflora') (*see* picture above)
6 Golden sage (*Salvia officinalis* 'Aurea')
7 Meadowsweet (*Filipendula ulmaria*)
8 Tarragon (*Artemisia dracunculus* 'Sativa')
9 Yarrow (*Achillea millefolium*)
10 Camomile (*Chamaemelum nobile*)
11 Artemisia (*Artemisia schmidtiana* 'Nana')
12 Santolina (*Santolina chamaecyparissus*)
13 Victoria sage (*Salvia farinacea*)
14 Lavender (*Lavandula angustifolia*)

Paving stones enable people to step right into the herb garden and smell the herbs or harvest them easily.

*Tarragon (*Artemisia dracunculus*) is a popular aromatic herb cultivated for its sweet, anise-like flavour.*

*Flowering onion (*Allium atropurpureum*) is an ornamental herb that provides stunning deep red-purple flower heads.*

Bird bath

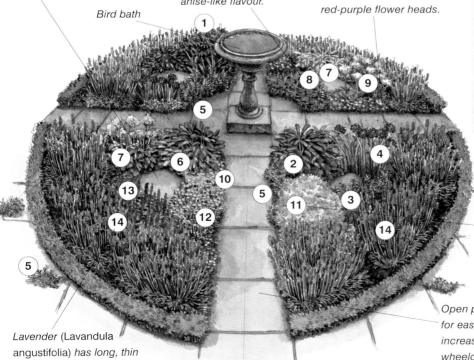

*Artemisia (*Artemisia schmidtiana*) has mounded cushions of ferny, silvery-grey leaves that make lovely edgings to a pathway.*

Open paved pathway to allow for easy access. Width can be increased to accommodate wheelchairs and walkers.

*Lavender (*Lavandula angustifolia*) has long, thin silver-grey leaves and pale lavender-blue blooms from spring until late summer.*

Project: planting a herb container

Herbs thrive on sunshine, so your herb container should get at least six hours of full sun a day in the growing season, and should also be easy to access. The next stage is to choose a selection of herbs – some of the many possibilities are chives, lavender, thyme, savory, tarragon and coriander (cilantro). With a little care, you can have fresh herbs all summer long to flavour your pasta, pizza, salads, meat and vegetables.

ABOVE *Select healthy herb starts and read the labels carefully so you understand the growth habits and required care.*

MATERIALS

- Large container with drainage holes
- Pea gravel, small rocks or broken crockery
- Potting compost (soil mix) with added garden compost and sharp sand or grit.
- Shovel or trowel to fill container
- Herbs such as chives, parsley, lavender, basil and oregano

GARDENER'S NOTE

Most herbs will produce their strongest flavour when grown in low-nutrient soil, but when closely planted in a container they will need a little more feeding than they would in the ground.

1 *Cover the bottom of the container with a layer of drainage material and fill it with compost.*

2 *Place the potted herbs on the container in their pots to lay out the proposed arrangement and spacing.*

3 *Turn the pot upside down, holding the plant with your index and third finger on each side of the stem. Tap the pot or squeeze it to release the plant.*

4 *If the plant is root bound, pull apart some root fibres to encourage new root growth direction. Plant each herb at the same level as it was at in its pot.*

5 *Continue to plant up the container until you have the balance you want. Keep the container well watered until the plants are established.*

FRUIT AND VEGETABLE GARDENS

If a productive garden is your choice, but you are not confident about whether you have the time and energy for managing vegetable beds, fruit vines and fruit trees, then here you will find low-maintenance ideas for growing fruit and vegetables. A section on Fruit Gardens demonstrates the many growing options, and shows that the most 'fruitful' planting approach is to choose varieties that suit your climate and situation. It also discusses how to integrate fruit in the garden to ensure a year-round harvest, practical advice for planting blueberries, raspberries and strawberries, as well as the dwarf, semi-dwarf, columnar and container fruit tree options for limited spaces or those with less energy.

Growing fresh vegetables and using them to cook with is a rewarding way of ensuring that your meals are made with healthy, organic produce. The stages from planting to harvest also provide great activities to share with grandchildren. As well as considering general principles, Vegetable Gardens includes projects for growing beans and cucumbers, potatoes, and a lettuce garden, and a plan for a raised-bed vegetable garden.

OPPOSITE *Harvesting runner (green) beans is a pleasurable activity for young and old – and will add extra flavour to home-cooked meals.*

ABOVE *If you love raspberries, choose your varieties so that you can harvest them from summer right through to the autumn.*

ABOVE *There is a tomato variety for every situation – grow them indoors, outdoors, in containers or in hanging baskets.*

ABOVE *Apple trees like a sunny, sheltered position – this will give the fruit an extended ripening time.*

FRUIT GARDENS

"Live each season as it passes: breathe the air, drink the drink, taste the fruit" are the words of American author and naturalist, Henry David Thoreau. Having access to seasonal, nutritious, sweet and juicy fruit from your own crops throughout the growing season is enormously rewarding. If you choose the fruit wisely, understand the potential and limitations of your growing zone and prepare the soil, then your efforts will reap a harvest of healthy and robust fruits all through the summer.

ABOVE *Hand picking berries is a rewarding way to spend time in the garden or in the berry field.*

GETTING BACK TO FRUIT BASICS

Years ago, you could tell the season simply by viewing the fresh fruit on display in your local grocery store. Today we are bombarded with almost any fruit at any time of the year. While some may regard this as a great way of ensuring a varied diet or, more likely, just accept it as the way things are, longtime gardeners are often disappointed by the perfect-looking berries or melons that are available in all seasons and that are dry and tasteless to eat. Indeed, one of the advantages of being a 'senior' is that we remember how fruit is supposed to taste!

Growing your own fruit guarantees that you'll have fresh and delicious produce, but make sure that you choose fruits that you (or your friends and family) like to eat, since you may get some big crops). If you love it, grow it. Homegrown fruits are also the central ingredients of other edibles that give extra flavour to our meals, especially when they are home-made – desserts, jams, jellies, wines and juices.

SEASONAL FRUIT HARVEST

The seasons of different fruits will influence your choice of what to grow. For instance, you may have several types of strawberry plants or raspberry canes that will welcome the early stages of summer into your garden store. So why not include some blueberry bushes whose fruits will ripen throughout the summer? You can add a small fruiting columnar tree, either apple or plum, or some autumn-fruiting raspberries – and then you have a delicious and accessible fruit garden to enjoy from early summer through to the autumn.

Before establishing a fruit garden, find out the best fruit varieties for your climate (the climate can dramatically affect the fruiting patterns) and the conditions in your garden. Don't forget that many fruits have early, mid- and late season ripening times so you can stretch your harvests out over the summer and into the autumn. There are several types of raspberries that ripen in the early days of summer as well as some varieties that will give you a second and longer fruiting yield later in the season.

OPPOSITE *A fig tree, redcurrants and a columnar pear tree on the trellis makes this garden corner a rich oasis of homegrown produce. For those in tropical climates, choose oranges, lemons and limes.*

LEFT *A garden full of fresh fruit delights: peaches, strawberries, apples, rhubarb, blackcurrants, raspberries and, in the foreground, a mass of blueberries.*

FRUIT PLANTING ESSENTIALS

Locating your garden fruit in or near the vegetable or flower garden will attract many of the pollinators needed for your fruit blossoms. Aim to plant in areas that are free from frost pockets, not exposed to winds and have good drainage. Also, select varieties with the least insect and disease problems. Small fruits thrive best in a fertile, sandy loam soil high in organic matter, but they will give good returns on average garden soil that has adequate fertilization and good cultivation practices.

If space is a limiting factor, small fruits can serve double duty as the ornamental showpieces in your garden. For example, apple trees (*Malus* spp.) provide as lovely spring blooms as any ornamental flowering specimen and will give you a delicious harvest of fruit that a strictly ornamental tree will not.

Likewise, consider using strawberries as a border for a flowerbed or as ground cover. Grapes and raspberries may be planted parallel to flower or vegetable gardens on a trellis or a fence. Plant blueberries to form a dense hedge, or use them as a foundation, planting around the home. You will have at least three seasons of attraction with these – and countless tasty desserts!

Successful home fruit growing should follow the best management practices throughout the year, which means a regular schedule of pruning, fertilizing, watering and pest control. Be assured, however, that the fruits listed in the plant directory (*see* pages 146–149) were selected because they are fairly low maintenance, take little space, and will thrive in containers.

ABOVE *Treat small container lemon trees with the same care as those in the ground – provide good drainage, regular watering, feeding, and high humidity.*

LEFT *A dwarf pear tree is a good choice because the fruit is easily accessible. The fruit will be ready to harvest in the late summer and early autumn.*

GROWING BLUEBERRIES

Blueberries are highly ornamental as well as productive. These attractive, airy shrubs produce lovely white, urn-shaped flowers in the spring. The blossoms turn into delicious, showy berries that decorate each branch with eye-catching shades of purple. Autumn is when these shrubs give us a leaf confetti display of maroons, purples, reds and oranges.

Highbush blueberries are the most popular, and they produce the largest, juiciest fruit, but they need a very acid soil. If you can't provide this, either in the garden or in a container, you could try the smaller-fruited rabbit-eye blueberries (*Vaccinium ashei*), which tolerate less acid and drier conditions.

Ideal planting conditions

If you are growing blueberries in the ground, put them where they have full sunlight for most of the day and where they are far enough from tree roots to avoid competition for moisture and nutrients. They will thrive in porous, moist, sandy, acidic soils high in organic matter. It's good practice to mulch them heavily with pine needles to increase the soil's acidity and keep it moist at all times, but ensure good drainage since they can't tolerate saturated soils.

Mulching is effective when planting blueberries. Many growers combine a layer of leaves at the bottom with 5–7.5cm (2–3in) of sawdust on top. Renewed annually, this heavy mulch retains moisture, keeps the soil cool and adds the required organic matter.

When your bushes are in their third year, you can prune them any time between autumn and either throughout spring or when the new growth appears. Pruning consists mainly of removing low-spreading canes and dead and broken branches. As the bushes mature and get larger, select six to eight of the most vigorous, upright-growing canes for fruiting wood, and remove all others.

Container blueberries

Blueberries thrive best in full sunlight. They also need a large container, so once it is filled and planted it will be heavy and difficult to move. If no part of your garden has enough direct sun, put the container on a wheeled holder so you can move the container easily and safely to ensure that the plant has maximum benefit from the sun.

Plant the blueberry in the container using ericaceous (lime-free) compost (soil mix) leaving a gap of 10cm (4in) below the top of the container for

ABOVE *A mass of ripe blueberries gets sweeter as they bask in the sun, almost ready to be picked.*

watering. Don't bury the plant any deeper than it was in its original container – blueberries have shallow roots and need to be kept at the surface. Water the plant thoroughly with collected rainwater, if possible, and immediately add a bit of light mulch over the top of the roots. The container mulch could be pine needles or coarse bark.

Blueberries need constant moisture, so water them regularly or, better still, provide a drip watering system. In hot weather, you'll need to water them every day. Rainwater is preferable since tap water tends to raise the alkalinity of the soil. They should be fed every month, starting in the spring. You can miss out a month of fertilizing in early to midsummer, but make sure you resume fertilizing them for another month after this. Then wait until the spring to start feeding them again.

FAR LEFT *Birds love ripe blueberries so protect your crop by covering the bush with fleece or netting.*

LEFT *White flowers shaped like upside-down urns let you know that the blueberry season is not far away.*

Project: planting blueberries in a container

You will need to plant young blueberry plants in very large containers, preferably the large, wooden planters that are used for small trees, since these cope well with changeable weather conditions. Make sure that there are plenty of drainage holes as blueberries do not like to have their roots sitting in water. If possible, plant at least two varieties to achieve optimal pollination and a longer harvest period.

ABOVE *Blueberry bushes produce fruit all through the summer if you choose early, mid-season and late fruiting varieties.*

MATERIALS

- Half a whiskey barrel or a container that has approximately 30 x 30 x 30cm (2 x 2 x 2ft) dimensions
- Two parts ericaceous (lime-free or acid) compost (soil mix) mixed with one part leafmould
- Blueberry plants (*Vaccinium* spp.): *V.* 'Sunshine Blue', *V.* 'Northsky', *V.* 'Bluecrop' and *V.* 'Earliblue' all grow well in containers
- Mulch mix – use an equal mixture of pine needles and leafmould
- Protective netting to give the plant protection from hungry birds. A bamboo or metal frame with netting over it can be used for a more permanent structure.

1 *Site your container in a location with a sunny exposure. Create your soil mix using leafmould and potting soil suitable for acid-loving plants.*

2 *Fill the container with the soil mix and pack the mix down firmly.*

3 *If roots are tightly bound, separate them gently. Plant the bush at the same level it was at in its pot.*

4 *Mulch the surface of the soil with a thin layer of leafmould and pine needles. Water well with rainwater.*

5 *When the berries start to form, cover the plant with light netting fabric to discourage marauding birds and squirrels.*

GROWING RASPBERRIES

Raspberries do better in cool temperatures than many soft fruits. They like sun but tolerate partial shade, and need a rich, moist, slightly acid soil. Train them on wires, fixed to stakes at each end of the row. They can become infected with viruses over the years, so when production falls off, usually after about 7–8 years, replace them with virus-free plants, preferably in a different part of the garden. Some varieties are more resistant than others.

There are two types of raspberry, summer-fruiting, which crop heavily over 2–3 weeks around midsummer, and autumn-fruiting (or ever-bearing), which produce fruit continuously from summer until the first frosts. In hot climes, autumn-fruiting ones may produce one crop in early summer on the lower canes, and a second in late summer or early autumn on the top ones. Cropping times depend on the variety: extend the summer-fruiting season by growing the early Glen Clova, for example, and later Malling Admiral. Other good summer varieties are Glen Ample and Tulameen; autumn varieties include Autumn Bliss, Joan J, Bababerry (tolerates hot summers) and Heritage.

LEFT *Raspberry canes tied to wire supports will make your care routine and harvest significantly easier and safer.*

PLANTING AND CARING FOR RASPBERRIES

In most climates, the best time to plant raspberries is as soon as the danger of frost has passed, typically in the early spring. Autumn planting is an option, unless your winters are very cold. Raspberries like soil that has ample compost and organic material worked in. Feed them once in spring and once in summer with a balanced fertilizer or well-rotted manure. Raspberries like 2.5–4cm (1–1½in) of water each week.

1 *Prepare the soil by taking out grass and weeds and spreading organic matter such as peat moss or aged manure to create a loose, porous soil.*

2 *Use garden rows 2.5–3m (8–10ft) long and 38cm (15in) wide. Use a line of string to guide the planting. Dig a hole the same depth and width as the roots.*

3 *Place the plant so that the point where the roots join the stem is 2.5cm (1in) below the soil. Backfill until the hole is three-quarters full. Water well.*

4 *Hammer in metal stakes, at least 1.5m (5ft) high once they have been installed. Attach 3 parallel lines of wire, evenly spaced about 2.5cm (1in) apart.*

GROWING STRAWBERRIES

Strawberry plants (*Fragaria* spp.) are versatile and can be grown in rows, mounds, containers and as a cover crop. They are among the most popular fruits.

There are two main types of strawberries: summer-fruiting, which crop heavily over 2–3 weeks in early or midsummer, and perpetual-fruiting (or ever-bearing), which crop briefly in summer and then over a longer period in autumn, or produce two or three flushes from spring to autumn, depending on the climate. The summer varieties are bigger, juicier and more tasty. There are also alpine strawberries, smaller but with a good flavour; and a recent development, day-neutral strawberries. These are unaffected by day length, so if they are kept warm enough (minimum 10°C/50°F) they will fruit at any time of year. Plant them successively from spring to autumn to ensure fruit almost all year round. However, they are smaller and less juicy and flavoursome than the other types.

The cropping period for summer-fruiting strawberries can be extended by growing early (such as Elvira, Earliglow, Honeoye), mid-season (Cambridge Favourite, Alice) and late varieties (Cambridge Late Pine, Domanil). Recommended perpetual-fruiting varieties are Aromel and Flamenco. Plant them in rows or mounds set 45cm (18in) apart. Remove the runners to keep the plant's energy going to the fruit. Water well on planting, and feed with a balanced fertilizer once new growth

appears, then again mid-season. To prevent weeds, retain moisture and keep the fruit off the ground, add a mulch of grass clippings, straw or sawdust around the plant's base. Ever-bearers will need 2.5cm (1in) of water each week during the growing season. When the fruit forms, place a straw layer around the plants, to keep the fruit off the ground and mud free. Replace plants with new stock every 2–3 years, preferably where strawberries have not been grown for at least 3 years. Using a rotation system ensures that there are always new plants at their best. Old plants should be destroyed, not composted, to prevent the spread of viral diseases.

ABOVE *Strawberry plants can easily be grown in grow bags on a wooden structure or in hanging baskets on a patio.*

BELOW *Strawberry rows can be planted with landscaping fabric that maintains moisture and reduces weeds.*

LEFT *For a higher yield, hand-pollinate strawberries by brushing up pollen from the stamens and dusting it over the stigmas.*

Design focus: an easy-access fruit garden

For most gardeners, tasting a sweet berry or juicy apple from their own garden is a delectable experience. This illustration shows an idea for a dedicated fruit garden that is easy to manage, a pleasure to look at and will ensure you a plentiful harvest all summer long. You don't have to interpret it literally – just borrow elements from it that appeal to you to fit within your own garden. So take inspiration from the ideas shown here, but the best advice is to grow fruit that you most love to eat.

Growing fruit in your garden is not difficult – you just need to know what varieties will do well in your climate and what cultivation techniques will help them mature. For example, blueberries are a popular and reliable fruiting shrub, but you need to know that they thrive in very acidic conditions.

Raspberries are low maintenance if they get enough sun, irrigation and wires to keep them in bounds. Growing strawberries in raised beds allows you to give them the slightly acid soil they like, if your garden soil is chalky, and also makes it easier to protect them from slugs. The berries here are chosen so that there is a variety ripening at any point in the season.

Several columnar apples have been developed that take up little space, are easy to maintain, yet produce tasty apples. Asian pear trees produce an abundance of juicy fruit and are typically pest-free and low-maintenance.

PLANTING LIST

1 Blueberry (*Vaccinium* spp.)
2 Asian pear tree (*Pyrus pyrifolia*)
3 Blackcurrant (*Ribes nigrum*)
4 Columnar apple tree (*Malus sylvestris* var. *domestica*)
5 Strawberry (*Fragaria virginiana*)
6 Gooseberry (*Ribes grossularia*) (see picture above)
7 Raspberry (*Rubus idaeus*)

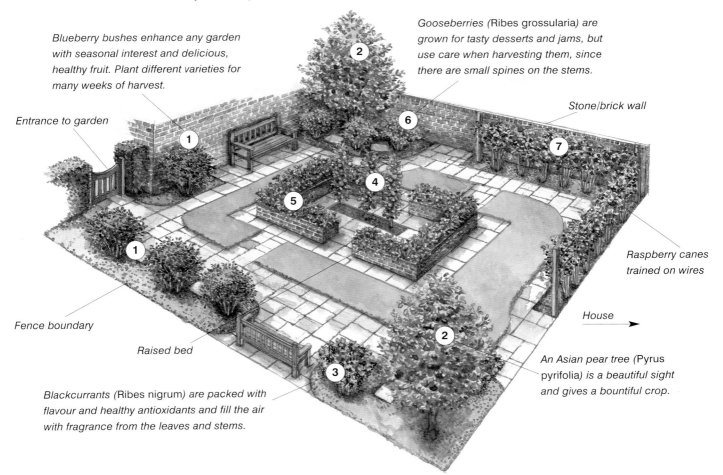

Blueberry bushes enhance any garden with seasonal interest and delicious, healthy fruit. Plant different varieties for many weeks of harvest.

Gooseberries (Ribes grossularia) are grown for tasty desserts and jams, but use care when harvesting them, since there are small spines on the stems.

Entrance to garden

Stone/brick wall

Raspberry canes trained on wires

House →

Fence boundary

Raised bed

Blackcurrants (Ribes nigrum) are packed with flavour and healthy antioxidants and fill the air with fragrance from the leaves and stems.

An Asian pear tree (Pyrus pyrifolia) is a beautiful sight and gives a bountiful crop.

Project: planting a strawberry urn

Strawberries are enjoyed for the colour they bring to the garden as well as their sweet taste. The strawberry urn has small side pockets or openings that hold the small plants, so that the roots have access to plenty of soil but the fruits are kept clean, not lying on the ground. The urn must have drainage holes in the bottom. When the planting is finished, be sure to position the urn in full sun.

ABOVE *In the fruiting season keep a careful eye on the maturing strawberries and pick them as soon as they are ripe.*

MATERIALS
- Strawberry urn in terracotta or plastic
- Potting soil mixture
- Pea gravel, small rocks or broken crockery
- Strawberry plants for each hole and additional ones for top surface. Many strawberry varieties are suited to containers (*see* those mentioned on page 67). Look for those that will thrive in your climate and are labelled by the manufacturer as virus free (strawberries are prone to viruses).
- 2.5cm (1in) PVC pipe drilled with holes
- Complete fertilizer

1 *If you have a terracotta urn, place the urn in a tub of water for about an hour, or alternatively wet the urn with a hose or watering can – if you don't do this the clay will wick the water out of the soil.*

2 *Put about 2.5cm (1in) of your soil in the bottom of the container and then cover this lightly with a layer of pea gravel, small rocks or broken crockery. This will help with drainage.*

3 *Fill the urn with soil until you reach the lowest level of pockets. Insert a plant in each of the lower pockets, filling around with soil and firming them in. The crown of the plants must be just above the soil level.*

4 *Water the lower level and each pocket. Then place the PVC pipe down the centre of the pot so that each plant will get adequate moisture. Fill with soil until the next level of pockets. Repeat the planting.*

5 *Stop adding soil when you get to 5cm (2in) below the rim. Add three to four plants in the top, and fill in with soil. In the growing season, water each plant, keeping the soil moist but not soggy.*

GROWING FRUIT TREES

Few things give more pleasure than being able to pluck a healthy apple or plum from your own tree.

As with any new plants, spend time researching the varieties of that will thrive in your climate. Select varieties with the least insect and disease problems. Talk to your local orchard group, horticultural society, agricultural extension or reputable nursery to learn about the trees that do well in your area. Usually the biggest limiting factor when selecting fruit trees is extreme winter conditions. But do your research and you can feel confident about adding a fruiting tree to your garden space.

Dwarf and semi-dwarf trees

Growing fruit need not be a lot of work if you choose the varieties carefully, and even in a small garden you are sure to find something that you can grow successfully. Most of the fruit

RIGHT *A fruit salad tree is truly a product of genetic science – it bears five to to eight different fruits of the same family on one plant.*

trees grown nowadays are grafted on to rootstocks that limit their growth to varying degrees. This is partly because of lack of space in gardens, and partly because, even for commercial growers, it is more difficult to pick fruit from very tall trees.

Small fruit trees are described as 'miniature' if they reach 1.8–2.4m (6–8ft) in height. Dwarf trees can grow between 2.4–3m (8–10ft), while semi-dwarfs reach 3.6–4.5m (12–15ft). They do have a reputation for being hard to keep healthy, and this is because they have shallow roots and are therefore vulnerable to water shortage. However, keep them fed and watered and the advantages (small size, earlier fruit, easy pruning and harvesting) outweighs any inconvenience.

LEFT *A dwarf peach tree (*Prunus persicus*) can grow in a container on your patio and will give lovely spring blossoms and tasty fruits later in the summer.*

BELOW *A columnar or 'pillar' apple tree is a great addition to a patio, deck, or other small area. Many accessible fruits form along short, spur-like branches.*

Columnar apple trees

As their name suggests, columnar apple trees have the shape of a column (although some people also liken them to bottle brushes), because they grow straight up and have a very small branch length. Growing to an average height of 2.4–3m (8–10ft) and 0.5m (2ft) wide, a fully mature columnar can grow and produce healthy fruit for about 20 years.

Fruit salad trees

Another relatively new option that will add more variety to your fruit crop is a single tree with multiple fruits, often called fruit cocktail or fruit salad trees. Most multiple-fruit trees are grafted on to pest-resistant rootstocks, but you should be careful about the size that these dwarf trees may reach. One version has a citrus theme, with oranges, mandarins, lemons, limes, grapefruit, tangelos and pomelos. Another has stone fruits such as peaches, apricots, plums, nectarines and peachcots. Other versions produce different types of apple, including red, green and yellow skin varieties, or different types of pear, called multi-nashis. Stone fruits, citrus and tropical varieties suit warm and temperate climates while cold climates can grow all types. They can require heavy yearly pruning and shaping to keep them manageable. These are not yet widely available in all parts of the world but are likely to grow in popularity.

Asian pear trees

The Asian pear, also known as the nashi pear, is a vertical grower that has clusters of white, scented flowers that appear in the spring. These trees need little pruning, but you should lightly shape your tree during its first few years. The fruit should be thinned to one or two per cluster, otherwise the tree will probably produce many small fruits and may perform poorly the following year.

The pears are round and are often mistaken for a yellow apple, yet their flesh is very crisp and their taste is a cross between an apple and a pear. Unlike other pears that need to ripen after harvesting for several days, these are at their best straight from the tree – they are already sweet and ripe, with a delicious, crunchy texture. These versatile pears can be used in recipes that require either apples or pears.

Container fruit trees

Most fruit trees can be grown in a large pot – with the exception of cherries, which need larger spaces. While the

ABOVE *Citrus trees are tropical, but with special care and protection from the cold they will survive in temperate climates.*

material of the container won't affect growth, remember that ceramic pots will crack where winters are cold and icy. The key requirement for any pot you choose is that it provides adequate drainage. Generally, you'll want to use a container that measures 45–60cm (18–24in) wide and about the same depth. Larger containers, such as half whiskey barrels, can also be used.

Fruit trees in pots should be grown in fertile soil with a third of the soil mix perlite or vermiculite to keep the soil

LEFT *The Asian pear tree* (Pyrus pyrifolia) *produces firm yet juicy, tree-ripened pears in the late summer and early autumn. They taste like a combination of an apple and a pear.*

from getting waterlogged. Use slow-release fertilizer pellets, or feed the tree every two weeks with small amounts of fish fertilizer. When fruit is on the trees, it is critical to keep them well watered. This keeps the trees healthy and prevents fertilizer build-up in the soil.

To ensure that your potted trees stay healthy and productive, they should be repotted every two years after the leaves have fallen. Once mature, prune the roots about 2.5cm (1in) every other year, then replace the tree in its pot with about 20 per cent new soil.

VEGETABLE GARDENS

"There is nothing … as satisfactory or as thrilling, as gathering the vegetables one has grown". This quote by Alice B. Toklas captures the exhilaration that many gardeners feel when harvesting their homegrown vegetables. For most gardeners, working in their home gardens growing vegetables such as tomatoes, beans and cucumbers has tremendous appeal. They are easy to grow and care for, fun to harvest and there's always plenty to share with others.

ABOVE *Vegetable gardens are both practical and beautiful – here we see squash blossoms and dark green kale.*

HOMEGROWN TRADITIONS

In times of hardship when food was scarce, such as during the Great Depression, growing vegetables was a necessity for many. Potatoes, cabbage, parsnips, carrots and winter squashes were all common crops that would sustain families throughout the winter during these periods. Then there were the Victory Gardens of World War II when citizens were encouraged to grow their own fruit and vegetables to increase self-sufficiency and reduce the need for widespread food transportation. During these times, gardens were planted in back yards, empty lots and urban rooftops and co-operatives were formed where homegrown varieties of fruit and vegetables were shared.

BELOW *A simple and small one-level raised bed is bursting at its seams with salad greens.*

We are facing similar trends now as the 'green' movement encourages us to grow our own food again and keep our lands fertile. Staying connected with our food source and eating locally is the new mantra for gardeners who are taking responsibility for the ways that we grow and distribute our food, both for the good of the environment and our own health.

Growing vegetables is also about sharing knowledge, and about self-sufficiency and independence.

You may already have experienced years of pleasure in growing good things to eat. In this case you have much to share with your children and grandchildren who may have grown up thinking that beetroot (beet) only comes out of a can and spinach from a frozen box. So use your life experience, no matter where you live or what space you may have to garden in, to mentor and enthuse those who might have skipped a generation of gardening. As you do this, you will keep your own roots close to the earth and its bounty as you tend and harvest your favourite vegetables.

IDEAL GROWING CONDITIONS

A productive vegetable patch requires more than six hours of sunlight for a successful yield, although leafier vegetables such as lettuce and spinach grow happily with less sunlight. You'll also need a good-quality soil and adequate drainage.

VEGETABLE CHOICES

Depending on your garden, you may need to choose vegetables that grow most successfully in a limited space, or those that can be easily managed with more limited physical abilities. There is a wide assortment of plants, often hybrids, that ripen more quickly and have a higher yield. We can also plan to counterbalance planting extremes in our gardens, from low-growing dwarf bushes to sun-loving vines.

Vegetables such as green beans are ideal to grow vertically – that is, climbing up stakes or structures – because they make the best use of a limited space. A climbing green-bean yield is two to three times more than a bush bean yield in the same space. Other choices that grow well vertically are butter (lima) beans, cucumbers, melons, peas, squash and tall-growing tomatoes.

If you are new to vegetables or prefer an easy-care option then you can focus on examples such as lettuce, radish, spinach, peas, onions and beetroot. Vegetables that require considerably more maintenance include kohlrabi, cauliflower, leeks, carrots celery or head lettuce.

OPPOSITE *Raised planting beds allow you to grow produce almost all the year round, even where there is no natural soil available. Create them with heavy timber planks and make an allowance for water to drain freely.*

COMPANION PLANTING

Old-style vegetable gardens, sometimes called kitchen gardens, were a mixture of vegetables, herbs and flowers. Today, as we try to reduce our use of chemicals in our gardening practices and strive to attract beneficial insects and wildlife, this type of garden design not only produces a beautiful looking garden but also helps to create an organic system called 'companion planting', which naturally helps to repel pests and diseases.

In general, aromatic plants such as onions, marigolds and tomatoes help to ward off harmful insects. Even particular colours, such as orange and bright yellows, are thought to repel some destructive flying insects. Planting marigolds or nasturtiums near cabbages, radishes, cucumbers and tomatoes helps protect them from their insect invaders. Some long-time gardeners believe that planting marigolds (the 'workhorse' of pest deterrents) around the entire vegetable garden provides a 'moat' of pungent aromas and bright colours that repels insects.

Another rule of companion planting is to include herbs freely among vegetable crops because they can adversely affect the population of destructive bugs. Chives and garlic deter aphids. Oregano, in the same way as marigolds, is a good all-purpose plant for repelling most insect pests. Rosemary effectively deters beetles that attack beans. So planting a family of basil, oregano, rosemary and chives among the tomato and pepper plants creates a natural way of keeping the insect population under control.

It can also be fun discovering the particular flowers that are beneficial companion plants in your kitchen garden.

Asters and chrysanthemums repel most insects and provide the late-season colour that many gardens lack as they move from summer into autumn. Petunias, which can tolerate heat, will protect beans. Tansy (*Tanacetum vulgare*) has a triple benefit by controlling Japanese beetles, squash bugs and ants. Geraniums, an old-fashioned favourite, are an effective general insect repellant. Finally, the shape of flower petals provides safe landing spots for beneficial insects, so plant companion plants that produce tubular, flat and bowl-shaped flowers.

We've now gained the folklore wisdom and the scientific data that support the importance of coexistence among some vegetables, flowers and herbs. Their abilities to ward off, repel and even confuse insects offer us more options in the varieties of plants we grow and the reduction of chemical use.

ABOVE *Nasturtium works as an effective companion for many plants, keeping away aphids, bugs, and pumpkin beetles, as well as maximizing growth and flavour.*

LEFT *Teeming with produce, this corner bed includes curly kale,* Hemerocallis *'Stella de Oro', strawberry, globe artichoke, French marigolds, Lollo rossa lettuce, fennel, red cabbage, corn and borage.*

Project: growing beans and cucumbers on a trellis

An effective way to maximize your gardening in a minimal space is to grow vegetables together. One idea for this is to plan a tall structure that acts as the central focus on which climbers scramble up. This project demonstrates how you can grow beans and cucumbers together in a small raised bed using either a pre-made teepee structure or one that is constructed with bamboo poles.

ABOVE *This teepee was constructed with nine bamboo poles, but ready-made teepees will reduce time and effort.*

MATERIALS
- Suitable in-ground space or raised bed
- Teepee structure or 7–9 bamboo poles with which to make one
- Twine, string or masking tape
- Seeds of your choice of climbing bean or cucumber variety (soak them the night before for quicker sprouting)
- Plant labels

1 *If you are building your own support structure, start by tying three of the poles together at the top with garden twine, string or masking tape to create a tripod formation. Tie on the other poles at the same point, plant the teepee firmly in the ground or raised bed, and wrap and knot the twine at the top and at stages down the poles to create a sturdy structure.*

2 *If you are using a ready-made teepee, simply open it out to create a circular base and push the legs into the soil. There should ideally be a 5cm (2in) margin around the perimeter.*

3 *Once the structure is solid and firm, plant the seeds (or seedlings) in a circle inside of the base of the teepee stakes. Put the beans on one half of the circular trellis and the cucumbers on the other. Water the seeds or seedlings well.*

4 *As the seedlings grow into longer stems, coax the stems to touch the poles. They will then start to climb up.*

5 *Continue to water them well and remain vigilant about encouraging their vertical growth habits in the early days.*

6 *In the summer you can harvest juicy cucumbers and succulent green beans. Pick them often to get the most tender ones.*

Project: growing potatoes in containers

Potatoes can be grown without a lot of fuss and they can easily be stored for later consumption. There are about 100 varieties of edible potatoes, either mature (maincrop) potatoes or new potatoes, which are harvested before they reach maturity. Growing smaller-variety potatoes in containers is fun, and a good project to do with children. Gathering them without having to bend over the ground makes this crop easy and pain-free to harvest.

ABOVE *The green tops of potatoes and the flowers make an attractive container plant as the tubers fill out.*

MATERIALS

- Plastic container or storage tub
- Drill or knife for puncturing holes
- Multipurpose compost (soil mix) with added garden compost and/or well-rotted manure (or other organic matter)
- Seed potatoes – the following varieties do well in containers: 'Yukon Gold' – small with golden skin and a rich, buttery taste. 'All Blue' – a blue to purple skin with blue flesh. The colour holds once cooked. 'Red Pontiac' – a red-skinned variety with creamy white flesh. 'Fingerling' – a yellow and small, finger-shaped potato.

1 *Select seed potatoes with at least two eyes and put them, with the eyes facing up, in a well-lit, airy, frost-free place until 2.5cm (1in) sprouts have grown. This should take about 6 weeks.*

2 *Use a 45–75-litre (12–20-gallon) plastic container or storage tub. Drill or puncture several holes in the bottom of the container for drainage.*

3 *Add a third of your potting mixture to the container. Space your potato sprouts on top of the soil about 13cm (5in) apart and at least 7.5cm (3in) away from the sides of the container.*

4 *Cover the potatoes with soil, adding more as they grow (keeping top leaves free). When the soil reaches 2.5–5cm (1–2in) from the top of the container, stop adding soil. Keep well watered.*

5 *When the potato plants turn yellow and lose leaves, it means the tubers are almost mature and can soon be harvested.*

Design focus: a raised-bed vegetable garden

As we age, we may want to avoid having a huge vegetable garden that needs care and attention from the first frost-free day to the first sign of frost in the autumn. This illustration shows how you can create a vegetable garden with a wide selection of produce that is also reasonably low maintenance. This is achieved with raised beds, which eradicate much of the bending and crouching work associated with vegetable maintenance and harvesting.

Having raised beds near the back door will give instant access to your salad garden. Raised beds lessen the strain of maintaining the produce, but when working on your beds you should still use body mechanics that avoid undue pressure being exerted on you, along with appropriate ergonomic tools.

From cold crops such as peas, kale and lettuce to heat-loving tomatoes, peppers and cucumbers, you can plan succession plantings to keep an all-summer-long supply of fresh and nutritious seasonal foods. You can also plant two vegetables in the same bed – radishes and carrots are a good pairing because radishes mature early, leaving room for the late sprouting carrots.

The illustration shows how to plant certain flowers or herbs nearby called companion plants (*see* page 74). These attract beneficial insects to the garden that pollinate and feast on aphids.

Benches are sited nearby so you can take rest breaks and enjoy seeing your produce reach full maturity.

PLANTING LIST

1 Climbing beans (*Phaseolus* spp.) (*see* picture above)
2 Potatoes (*Solanum tuberosum*)
3 Marigolds (*Calendula officinalis*)
4 Onions (*Allium cepa*)
5 Radishes (*Raphanus sativus*)
6 Carrots (*Daucus carota*)
7 Beetroot (beet) (*Beta vulgaris* subsp. *vulgaris*)
8 Chard (*Beta vulgaris* subsp. *cicla* var. *flavescens* 'Northern Lights')
9 Lettuce (*Lactuca sativa*)
10 Peppers (*Capsicum* spp.)
11 Summer squash (*Cucurbita pepo*)
12 Peas (*Pisum sativum*)
13 Tomatoes (*Lycopersicon esculentum*)
14 Borage (*Borago officinalis*)
15 Basil (*Ocimum basilicum*)

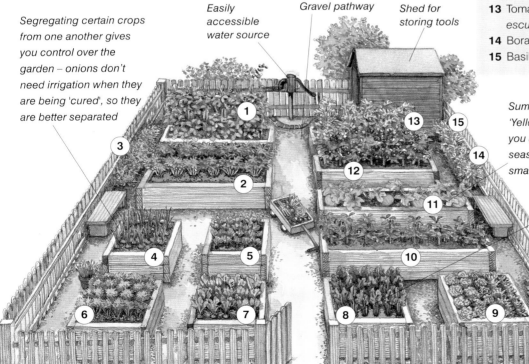

Segregating certain crops from one another gives you control over the garden – onions don't need irrigation when they are being 'cured', so they are better separated

Easily accessible water source

Gravel pathway

Shed for storing tools

Summer squash, especially the 'Yellow Crookneck' variety, will give you a steady crop throughout the season – pick them while they are small and tender.

Chard is a versatile and healthy green that can be eaten raw or cooked. One of few greens that rarely goes to seed, it is almost always available for your table.

Project: creating a lettuce garden in a container

Raising your own blend of greens is easy and cost-effective. As well as being convenient, growing leaf lettuces in a container is a way of keeping pests at bay. Position the container where it gets at least four hours of direct sunlight. If need be, put the container on a wheeled dolly so it can be moved to follow the sun. By choosing early and late varieties, you can have fresh salad greens for several months.

ABOVE *Choose varieties of lettuce with burgundy foliage, interesting edges, textures and different flavours.*

MATERIALS
- Young lettuce plants. To achieve maximum colour and texture in your planting choose from the following varieties:

  Early season:
  'Arctic King', 'Black-seeded Simpson', 'Grand Rapids' or 'Winter Marvel'

  Mid-season:
  'Red Fire', 'Freckles', 'Royal Oak Leaf' or 'Salad Bowl'

  Late season:
  'Diamond Gem', 'Esmerelda', 'Galactic' or 'Rosalita'
- Container with good drainage
- Pebbles
- Loose, fertile, sandy loam that is rich in organic matter

1 *Find a container that is not too deep (lettuce has shallow roots). Add a layer of pebbles at the base to aid soil drainage.*

2 *Fill the container with loose, fertile, sandy loam. The soil should be well-drained, moist, but not soggy.*

3 *Loosen the young plants from their pots, then place them on the soil at the spacing recommended for the variety.*

4 *Plant each seedling, at the same depth as it was in the pot, and firm in gently.*

5 *Keep the plants moist but not sodden. When harvesting, select your lettuce leaves from the outside of the plant.*

GARDENS WITH ADAPTABLE FEATURES

Having an age-proof garden means doing the things you have always loved in pretty much the same way, but making the mechanism simpler and more accessible. So the emphasis here is on features that make life easier for those needing convenient access.

Each of the four sections in this chapter – Patio Gardens, Raised-Bed Gardens, Vertical Gardens and Indoor Gardens – has flexible options to reduce the strain of associated gardening activities. Keeping a patio garden, with small beds, lightweight containers and a firm, level ground, may, in fact, be all that's required. Alternatively, raised beds are an ideal solution for those who have trouble bending or kneeling, and designs include constructions using brick, wood, hay bales or those built in kit form. Vertical gardens, the next section, explains the features that use the same ease-of-access principle as raised beds – including flower pouches, vertical baskets, trellises, teepees, arches, and pergolas. Finally, Indoor Gardens shows how having houseplants is a way of keeping in touch with nature in its myriad forms, without having to set foot outside.

OPPOSITE *This raised bed is simply constructed from wooden blocks, and is situated on a non-slip, level patio surface.*

ABOVE *Patio containers are easy to manage, and can be enjoyed to the full when placed right next to seating areas.*

ABOVE *These terracotta pots are suspended on a trellis fence with lightweight plant holders – an instant vertical garden.*

ABOVE *A sunny doorway will accommodate a houseplant, one way to bring the life of a garden into your home.*

PATIO GARDENS

From the open terraces in Italy overlooking the ripening grapevines to the private walled gardens in New York City, we all appreciate that area where the outdoors and the indoors meet, creating a unique garden experience. This area of outdoors offers us tranquillity, rest, fresh air, sun and – best of all – a place never more than a few steps from our door. As we age and look to economize on garden space and effort, patio gardens might be just what we need.

ABOVE *A chair placed in a shady spot on a sturdy, level surface creates a perfect and tranquil garden experience.*

BRINGING THE PATIO TO LIFE

A well-planned patio garden makes the most of a small space. If yours lacks in-ground garden beds, then adding a few containers will make a world of difference to any hard-landscaped area.

Raised beds are another option – small trees, shrubs and even berry bushes can thrive in raised beds and will enhance the atmosphere.

Consider the view you will have from indoors when the weather is inclement. Watching a small maple tree change colour in the autumn or bright daffodil heads nodding in a container gives a sense of well-being when observed through the window.

PRACTICAL CONSIDERATIONS

For anyone who is unsteady on their feet, walks with support or is wheelchair bound, the hard walking surface should be level, smooth and non-skid. If it is made of concrete, colour or tint the cement to avoid reflective glare. Other surfaces, such as bricks or pavers, are good flooring choices, but they should adhere to the requirements above.

It's important that a wheelchair or walker can easily navigate in and out of the doors, so make sure you have an easy knob or door latch to operate. In addition, manual doors should be lightweight so they are easy to open – a heavy door makes it much harder to

access the garden. If required, check that the doorway dimensions accommodate a wheelchair or walker, and don't overlook the threshold, which needs to be as level as possible with little or no elevation to deal with when moving across it.

Provide good lighting in the patio so you can safely enjoy the warm evenings outside. Automatically timed lighting is a safe and practical feature, or select a motion detector light that will illuminate the patio as you enter.

OPPOSITE *Beautiful tiles such as these can make the patio floor a striking feature to set off the plants.*

ABOVE *Create a small 'room' in a corner of the patio where you can slip away to read and enjoy a cup of coffee.*

LEFT *Lush plantings and overflowing containers on a patio make a lovely place to sit and relax.*

RIGHT *Sturdy containers full of aromatic herbs and long-lasting flowers can adorn a patio all year round.*

EASY PATIO GARDENING

As we have already discovered, enabling gardeners with physical limitations often involves thinking around a problem, and there is usually more than one option. Using lightweight containers to house your patio plants will, for example, let you move plants around to follow the sun or to rearrange the design. Another successful idea is to raise heavy containers on wheeled caddies, lightweight structures that allow easy movement around the garden.

Think about having a hanging basket or two, as they take up no ground space and can adorn any less than attractive blank walls with colourful, cascading flowers. It's a good idea to install an easy pulley system so you can lower and raise the baskets to maintain them.

Make sure you grow some herbs close to the doorway so you can quickly snip a few leaves when you are preparing a meal. A good patio also needs a few comfortable but stable chairs and a small table so you can spend time outdoors and enjoy the natural world around you.

Having a convenient water source is critical to keep your patio plants irrigated. Keep a short, lightweight hose or small watering can nearby to make irrigating your patio garden easy. Place a waterproof box on the patio for your tools, gloves and sunscreen so they are handy but not unsightly.

ABOVE *Hanging baskets create long-lasting confections of flowers and foliage.*

LEFT *A wide doorway in this Victorian-style conservatory leads on to a terrace. Period-style wirework and cast-iron containers complement the planting.*

Design focus: a patio garden for sanctuary and relaxation

A patio can be a private and restorative personal space. Being a manageable size, it requires less physical effort than a large garden to maintain. What is more, it can have ready access to the indoors and sturdy, level surfaces for easy and safe mobility. This illustration shows an enclosed set-up with a table and chairs for summer meals and refreshments. The design could be adapted around other patio formats: a garden corner, a front entrance walkway or a driveway or parking space.

The advantage of patios for senior gardeners is that they have a hard ground surface, creating a sturdy and secure base for those with unsteady feet or balance problems. The surface here has wide, level, square pavers with a contrasting brick pattern that invites you into the space. A similar material is used to define the parameters of the patio.

A selection of year-round plants are suggested here, all relatively easy to maintain. You can also add decorative containers, hanging baskets or wall planters. The symmetrical design is easy on the eye and the wide walkways, the wheeled hose holder and lack of clutter mean that there are no potential tripping hazards.

The simple water feature adds soothing trickling sounds and attracts birds and butterflies. If you have in-ground beds or raised beds, then small deciduous trees such as 'Little Gem' magnolias can be included, along with evergreen shrubs. With all these options, your patio will undoubtedly be an individual statement.

PLANTING LIST

1 Hinoki cypress (*Chamaecyparis obtusa* 'Gracilis')
2 Hinoki cypress (*C. o.* 'Nana Gracilis Glauca')
3 Shrub rose (*Rosa glauca*)
4 Lavender (*Lavandula*)
5 Daylily (*Hemerocallis* 'Stella de Oro')
6 English marigold (*Calendula officinalis*)
7 Sasanqua camellia (*Camellia sasanqua* 'Setsugekka')
8 Vine maple (*Acer circinatum*)
9 Japanese andromeda (*Andromeda* 'Temple Bells')
10 Sweet box (*Sarcococca confusa*)
11 Lady's mantle (*Alchemilla mollis*)
12 Christmas fern (*Polystichum acrostichoides*)
13 Cyclamen (*Cyclamen hederifolium*)
14 Japanese maple (*Acer palmatum*)
15 Busy Lizzy (*Impatiens* 'Dazzler White')
16 Plantain lily (*Hosta fortunei*)
17 Climbing hydrangea (*Hydrangea anomala*) (*see* picture above)
18 Little Gem magnolia (*Magnolia grandiflora* 'Little Gem')
19 Euonymus (*Euonymus fortunei*)

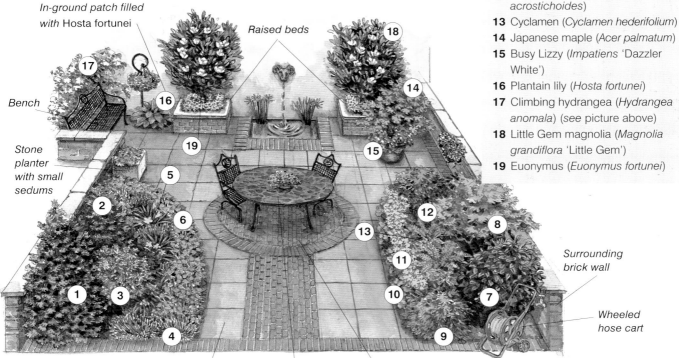

In-ground patch filled with Hosta fortunei

Raised beds

Bench

Stone planter with small sedums

Surrounding brick wall

Wheeled hose cart

Large pavers

Table

Brick patio surface

Project: planting a hanging basket

Using a wire mesh basket as a hanging container for plants allows you to plant not only on the top but also through the sides of the container, camouflaging the base of the basket and giving it a generously overflowing and luxurious look from below. A solid plastic container will not achieve this effect, because you can't plant through the sides. Good news – this basket can be reused each year!

ABOVE *The plants in this basket will soon grow to create a waterfall of colourful flowers and foliage.*

MATERIALS

- Wire basket 35–45cm (14–18in) diameter with a fibre or moss liner
- Scissors or pruners
- Compost (soil mix) (add slow-release fertilizer for a boost)
- Bedding plants in 5cm (2in) pots. Choose from trailing petunias, such as the 'Supertunia', 'Wave' or 'Surfina' series, busy Lizzies (*Impatiens* spp.), ivy geranium (*Pelargonium peltatum*), sweet potato vine (*Ipomoea batatas*), fuchsia (*Fuchsia* x *hybrida*), sweet alyssum (*Lobularia maritima*), trailing lobelia (*Lobelia erinus*), lemon verbena (*Aloysia citriodora*), water hyssop (*Bacopa monniera*) and *Lantana* spp.

1 *Use scissors or pruners to slice through the fibre liner to make the holes. To get full flower coverage stagger the rows. They need to be large enough to pull the plant through but snug enough to hold it firmly.*

2 *Fill the basket with compost to just below where the holes begin. Remove the plant from its cell and, from the outside of the basket, push the roots towards the centre of the container.*

3 *Add more plants so that the growth flows through the side. Add soil to cover the roots and repeat until you reach the top.*

4 *Add more soil to within 2.5cm (1in) of the rim and set 3–4 more plants on the top. Water thoroughly to settle the soil.*

5 *Hang the basket, getting help if necessary – or get someone to do it for you. When irrigating, use a watering wand.*

Project: planting a lightweight container

If you don't have the strength or flexibility to lift heavy containers, the best plan is to decide where you want them and put them in place before planting them up. However, sometimes containers need to be moved – you may be growing tender shrubs that cannot survive outdoors over winter, or perhaps you want to give prominence to seasonal displays. Wheeled trolleys are useful, but it still makes the job easier if the pot is not too heavy.

ABOVE *A small hand trowel and healthy flowers are some of the essentials needed to plant your container garden.*

MATERIALS

- Plastic or fibreglass container at least 45cm (18in) in diameter, with drainage holes
- Lightweight fabric
- Recycled polystyrene beads (mailer pellets)
- Compost (soil mix)
- A mixture of tall, filler and trailing plants. Tall options: canna, colocasia, false cypress (*Chamaecyparis obtusa*) and palm lily (*Cordyline*); filler options: basil (*Ocimum basilicum*), coleus (*Solenostemon*), blood-leaf (*Iresine herbstii*) and Swiss chard (*Beta vulgaris*); trailing options: million bells (*Bidens calibrachoa*), creeping zinnia (*Schizanthus pinnatus*), lobelia and nasturtiums (*Tropaeolum*).

1 *Line the base of the pot with fabric. Fill the pot a third full with polystyrene beads. This will bulk out the volume of the pot without adding to its weight. Then fill with compost to within 2.5cm (1in) of the rim.*

2 *Place the taller plant either in the centre or towards the back of the container, depending on whether the pot is to be viewed from all sides, or put against a wall.*

3 *Plant trailing plants around the edges where they will cascade over the sides of the container to hide the hard edges.*

4 *Set the other plants around the central one, filling in the spaces and mixing varieties of colour and shapes.*

5 *Water the pot until you see water seeping out of the bottom. Keep it watered, fed and groomed throughout the season.*

Project: making a fragrant window box

A window box spilling over with sweetly scented flowers and aromatic foliage will be a delight, from inside and out, and will bring you hours of rewarding scents – and natural aromatherapy. Choose a few strongly-scented varieties that you know you will love, but combine them with some non-scented ones to add colour – otherwise the mixture of fragrances might be overpowering.

ABOVE *A colourful and densely planted window box gives a cheerful welcome to friends and neighbours.*

MATERIALS

- A selection of plants of various heights – used here are scented geraniums (*Pelargonium* spp.), trailing nasturtiums (*Tropaeolum majus*), sweet alyssum (*Lobularia maritima*), ivy (*Hedera helix*) and heliotrope (*Heliotropium arborescens*)
- Window box with drainage holes
- Coffee filter or old piece of wire mesh to cover the drainage holes
- Compost (soil mix)

GARDENER'S NOTE

Other possibilities not included in this project are lavender, dianthus, petunias and trailing sweet peas.

1 *Select your plants by arranging them in a pattern of two or three rows. Put the taller flowers at the back and graduate the heights with the trailing plants at the front.*

2 *Place the coffee filter or screening in the bottom of the window box. This will prevent the compost from falling out through the holes.*

3 *Fill the window box about two-thirds full with compost, and firm it down gently.*

4 *Following your window box planting design, place the plants one at a time in their allocated positions, filling in with compost as you go.*

5 *Add compost to surround the roots, and gently tamp the compost to remove air pockets. Keep doing this as you plant until the level is about 2.5cm (1in) below the top of the window box. Water well.*

RAISED-BED GARDENS

Raised beds are not new. A similar concept was used in the Hanging Gardens of Babylon to create tiers of flowers, and medieval monks used them to cultivate food and herbs. Yet more than any other gardening invention the raised bed has revolutionized the lives of gardeners. Besides providing easy access for those who have problems with bending and flexibility, they have multiple benefits, ranging from the reduction of soil compaction to greater productivity.

ABOVE *This raised bed is built of solid timber lengths that are intersected to create stability and a solid, natural effect.*

ADVANTAGES OF RAISED BEDS

They come in all shapes and sizes. Like clothes, you can buy them 'off the rack' or you can use your creative and mechanical skills to design your own. Raised beds can make a garden accessible to those with limited physical mobility or with low vision, and they add beauty to any garden. Having a raised garden bed also gives you more control in your choice of location and soil quality, and makes it easier to reduce pests. They are undoubtedly a great solution for the smaller urban garden or senior facility.

Probably the most significant advantage to a raised bed is that it minimizes the need to bend over to plant, weed and harvest. In most cases, you can decide the height of your bed so you can make it as comfortable as possible.

Raised beds also enable you to improve the quality of your soil. This will allow you to grow the plants you want, even if the soil in your garden is not suitable. However, if your soil is very chalky, and you are growing acid-loving plants, you might need to lay a barrier at the bottom of the bed to separate the chalky from the more acidic soil.

Because the sides of raised beds are exposed to the sun, the soil warms up more quickly in the spring. This means that you can plant things earlier and, with the soil staying warm throughout the growing season, flowers and vegetables have the advantage of more time to flourish and ripen.

A critical feature of a healthy garden is good drainage. Because the soil in a raised bed is higher than any place water would naturally settle, you can be assured of adequate drainage. In addition, practically speaking, the advantage of raised beds over in-ground rows is that you can work in wet weather without compacting the garden soil and getting your feet muddy.

If you introduce at least one raised bed in your garden space you will see how it improves the quality of your gardening experience. The following pages show you how to build your own from scratch or put one together from a kit. There are many materials that can be used for raising beds, and it's fun and interesting to see how creative you can be!

LEFT *Raised beds not only provide a place to grow all kinds of different plants, they also offer us the best seat in a garden as they bring us close to the trees and flowers.*

RIGHT *Keeping your garden shipshape and undertaking general care and maintenance routines is most easily done if you can sit comfortably as you work, without bending over.*

OPPOSITE *A well-built raised bed can take on different roles, such as both a flower garden and an orchard. So it becomes a mini-garden with complementary elements.*

Design focus: raised beds

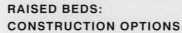

The raised-bed garden illustrations here show some of the many materials that can be used for constructing raised beds – wood, pre-made pavers, hay bales, natural stone and brick. While these represent some of the most commonly used materials, the options are endless – more ideas are shown in the panel below right. If your bed is on an in-ground base, you can also plant ground-hugging greenery along the edges to soften and naturalize the structure.

The width of a raised bed should allow you to reach the centre without strain – so no more than 90cm (3ft) if you can access from only one side and 150cm (5ft) if you have two-sided access.

If you are using or making several beds, the path between can be as narrow as 60cm (24in). To avoid mud forming, top the path with fine gravel, or add paving stones.

Because of its long life and ability to resist decay, pressure-treated wood might seem to be ideal for raised beds. If you decide to use treated wood, however, make sure that you get a type that is arsenic-free.

Whatever your needs, raised beds such as these offer an easier, more versatile, more comfortable and safer way to garden than in-ground beds.

RAISED BEDS: CONSTRUCTION OPTIONS

1. Simple wooden raised bed
2. Kit raised bed
3. Paver raised bed
4. Hay-bale raised bed
5. Tall raised bed
6. Raised stone or brick flower bed

ALTERNATIVE MATERIALS

7. Simulated wood planking
8. Railway sleepers (*see above*)
9. Breeze (cinder) blocks
10. Old car tyres stacked together
11. Sturdy, tall, soil-filled plastic bags
12. Galvanized metal water troughs
13. Soil mounds tamped at the edges, with mulch to stabilize the form.

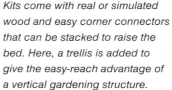

This basic bed can be raised two or three levels by using taller posts and additional boards. Top boards have here been added for seating.

Kits come with real or simulated wood and easy corner connectors that can be stacked to raise the bed. Here, a trellis is added to give the easy-reach advantage of a vertical gardening structure.

Real or simulated pavers can be stacked to the desired height.

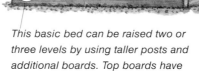

Grouped hay bales allow for a central growing area that is filled with soil as well as planting in the tops of the bales.

This style allows the gardener to stand when tending plants. Leg heights can be altered to allow a wheelchair gardener to get close.

Natural stone makes attractive beds that can be laid out in any shape or size. Brick can be used in the same way.

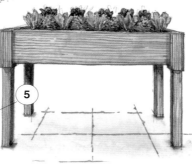

Project: making a raised bed out of bricks

This raised bed is shaped to fit a corner of the garden. You might not want to do this yourself, but understanding the stages will help you plan where your bed should be sited and the exact dimensions required, before commissioning someone to do it. Obviously the height can be varied according to your requirements. Similarly, as your interests or energy change, the plantings in this raised bed can be easily adjusted for variety.

ABOVE *Concrete or brick raised beds are durable and permanent. They will give you years of consistent access to your plants.*

MATERIALS
- Pointed stake
- Fine sand or line marker paint
- Spade
- Concrete mix
- Bricks and mortar
- Spirit level
- Pointing trowel
- Waterproof paint
- Rubble
- Gravel or pea shingle
- Topsoil
- Good potting medium

1 *Mark out the bed using a stake. Define the lines with fine sand. Dig out along the markings to a depth and width of 15cm (6in). Fill in with concrete to within 5cm (2in) of the top. Firm and leave for 24 hours.*

2 *Build up four or five courses of bricks, and set them into mortar, carefully checking the horizontal surfaces with a spirit level at each stage.*

3 *Clean up the mortar while wet with a pointing trowel. Leave to harden. Before filling with soil, coat with waterproof paint.*

4 *Add a layer of rubble topped with gravel for drainage. Fill in with topsoil and stir in a top layer of potting medium.*

5 *The completed raised bed is here planted with a selection of culinary herbs and wild strawberries.*

BREEZE-BLOCK BEDS

One option for constructing raised beds is to use breeze (cinder) blocks. The technique is to lay levels of blocks with the holes facing up. Work from the corners, ensuring the blocks are touching, and eliminate any gaps. Successive layers should be staggered – use two or three layers depending on the required height.

Fill the block holes around the side of these beds with soil, and plant herbs or drought-resistant plants to conceal the blocks and flow over the edge. Alternatively, cap the blocks to make a seat. The area enclosed by the blocks can be filled and planted as above.

RIGHT *The spaces in the top blocks can be planted with drought-resistant plants.*

Project: building a wooden raised bed

While building from a kit is the easiest way to make a raised bed (see page 96), doing it from scratch isn't complicated. Here is a simple raised bed made with cedar wood and screws. It is constructed upside down and inverted so the vertical posts that are still visible are secured in the ground. Here, three layers of wood raise the height to 45cm (18in), which will suit a wheelchair. Make it yourself if you are active, or ask someone to do it for you.

ABOVE AND OPPOSITE *Wooden raised beds can be narrow (above) or wider to allow for seating (opposite).*

MATERIALS

- 2.5m (8ft) long, 50 x 100mm (2 x 4in) piece of wood (for the corner posts and for the end pieces)
- 6 x 2.5m (8ft) long, 50 x 150mm (2 x 6in) pieces of wood for the sides and ends
- 48 x 90mm (3in) wood screws
- Hand or power saw
- 4 stakes for marking corners
- Post-hole digger
- Drill

GARDENER'S NOTE

You can adjust the height of the bed according to your requirements by changing the number of layers.

1 *Cut the 50 x 100mm (2 x 4in) pieces into four 60cm (2ft) tall corner posts. Cut three of the 50 x 150mm (2 x 6in) pieces in half for the ends. Assemble on a flat surface.*

2 *Mark the corners with the stakes. Dig four holes wide enough for the 50 x 100mm (2 x 4in) corner posts, and deep enough to fit the excess length of the posts.*

3 *Set one of the corner posts on its thin edge, and secure a 1.2m (4ft) 50 x 150mm (2 x 6in) post at one end with the screws. Repeat at the other end. Use a spare bit of wood beneath to protect the work surface.*

4 *Stand one of the end pieces up with the excess on top and attach 2.5m (8ft) 50 x 150mm (2 x 6in) pieces at the end of the construction in three layers.*

5 *Repeat at the other end, and repeat for the two long sides. Then invert the bed construction so that the excess length of the corner posts fits in the dug holes.*

Project: making a raised bed from a kit

You can buy modular systems for creating your own raised bed. With these kits almost everything is pre-cut, pre-measured and relatively simple to assemble. By using the corner pieces that join the sides together, you can put up a modular raised bed in very little time. Some kits allow you to adapt the height. They may be made of wood or recycled plastic, which is lightweight and won't rot or break.

ABOVE *The corner is created by adding the second base board. They are designed to snap in firmly.*

GARDENER'S NOTE

Before you start assembly, measure the area where the raised bed will be located so that it matches the dimensions of the modular kit you are using. If there is existing lawn on the area you will need to remove it by skimming off the turf and exposing the soil beneath.

Level the measured area and then lay a weed barrier – either fabric or a layer of cardboard or newspaper where the structure will sit. If the kit is light enough you can assemble it elsewhere and carry it across to your site (as shown here).

1 *Kits use dowels, metal pins or corner braces to 'lock' them in place. Here, a corner brace slots into the board. Use the four corner units to join the base boards.*

2 *In this way the raised bed starts to take shape. Ensure that the base remains stable as you work through the manufacturer's instructions.*

3 *This modular system can be built up as high as you require. Here, a second level of boards are being added.*

4 *Once the bed is in position, lay your weed barrier. For a deep bed you can fill the base of the bed with plastic bottles to bulk out the area (reducing the soil required).*

5 *Cover the bottles at the base of the bed with a plastic sheet with drainage holes, or landscaping fabric. You are now ready to fill your raised bed with the soil mixture.*

Project: irrigating a wooden raised bed

Raised beds have a tendency to dry out, so they need more watering than beds in the ground. Having a water source close to the bed makes irrigating them easier. Combining a soaker hose and a regular hose with a hose connector is a good solution, because this saves effort and minimizes waste. Soaker hoses come in a variety of sizes, so choose the length according to that of your raised bed.

ABOVE *Beans and corn are getting their water needs met by a soaker hose snaking its way through the raised bed.*

MATERIALS

- Pencil
- Drill
- Garden hose
- Soaker hose
- Two- or three-way hose connector valve with built-in shut-offs
- 3–4 female hose couplings
- U-shaped wire hose holders

GARDENER'S NOTE

This technique can be adapted for use with a non-wooden raised bed, either by drilling through the material of the bed to make the same hole for the hose to pass through, or by placing the soaker hose at the top of the bed.

1 *Mark on your frame where the entry point of the irrigation hose should be. In one end of the raised bed, drill a hole 5cm (2in) below the top of the raised bed, just large enough to accommodate a hose.*

2 *Calculate the lengths of hose required to cover the distance from the raised beds to the connector and from the connector to the water source. Cut the hose into shorter lengths to suit these calculations.*

3 *Using female hose couplings, attach two pieces of hose to the connector valve. These join one or more hoses to the tap, or to each other. A shut-off valve in each connector arm allows you to redirect the water.*

4 *Insert the other ends of the short hoses through the holes. Inside the raised bed, attach the short pieces of hose to the soaker hose. Attach another length of hose outside using a female hose coupling.*

5 *Arrange the soaker hoses in an S-shape to distribute the water. Place them at the base of the plants in the row so that water is distributed evenly over the roots. You can also bury them beneath the soil.*

VERTICAL GARDENS

Most plants grow vertically as they stretch towards the sun. A garden with vertical elements makes the most of this upward-growing journey of living forms. This approach will maximize space in a small garden and also provide easy maintenance options. Another vertical solution is to use elements in a hanging or raised form, so that plants can tumble downwards, or planted containers can be placed in a shelved structure to create an attractive display and easy watering access.

ABOVE *A tiered, mesh basket structure such as this allows you to be creative in your planting choices.*

PRACTICAL CONSIDERATIONS

Growing plants vertically means that much of your gardening can be done standing up, putting less pressure on your back. Vertical structures also make the most of a limited space and reduce the energy required to care for the garden. Vertical growth also makes it easier to spot problems with pests and diseases – with plants comfortably viewed at eye level.

As well as the obvious ease of access that vertical features bring, growing plants on structures that keep them tall and heading skywards is also a great way to fill less attractive garden areas, such as blank dividing walls and dark corners that may have been bare and neglected.

Growing plants up and over arbours or trellises can create shady areas, and a cool refuge away from the sun. You will need a heavy structure such as a metal arbour to support wisteria or three-leaf akebia (*Akebia trifoliata*).

Formal wooden obelisks can add style and elegance to a garden or, at the other end of the scale, try using a rustic handmade teepee made with bamboo, willow twigs or recently pruned fruit branches.

When planning vertical elements you can use the structure of existing walls and fences to train your plants, or take advantage of the various freestanding support structures available. Three examples of each are illustrated overleaf, along with other alternatives.

OPPOSITE *A wooden arbour offers a pathway to the sun for climbing roses and a perfect spot for a hanging basket.*

ABOVE *Grapevines clothe the whole of the porch structure, giving the area natural shelter and protection from the harsh sun.*

LEFT *Bent willow twigs create an airy and inviting arbour that lends support to lightweight climbing sweet peas.*

CONTAINERS

Breaking up the horizontal perspective of gardens and gaining a height variation is an important design dynamic, with the additional benefit that planting features are more accessible to those who have problems bending. One technique is to add a simple trellis to a pot, giving you a double-impact feature with flowers cascading to the ground and a climbing plant stretching upwards toward the sun.

Another idea is to group containers of various heights. Enhance this by planting a small tree or shrub with an upright growth habit. Make sure that the base is wide and stable. Recommended plants are Japanese holly (*Ilex crenata* 'Sky Pencil') and dwarf alberta spruce (*Picea glauca*).

BELOW *Stacking old tyres creates a practical and whimsical herb, flower or vegetable garden.*

ABOVE *Flower pouches are an easy and economical way to cover a blank wall with a cascade of colour.*

HANGING BASKETS

Another attractive vertical feature is hanging flower baskets that can be used to frame doorways, windows, porches and balconies, thereby combining a dramatic selection of flowering and cascading plants in a restricted area.

You can gain significant height variety in the garden by using baskets and containers at different levels. A successful hanging basket can have tall, spiky plants that are complemented by masses of cascading plants. Wise placement of your baskets will ensure that you get to enjoy the full visual effect of a well-planted container.

The baskets need to be accessible so you can water and deadhead the plants. Pulley systems are available that move the plants to your level. Recommended plants are sweet potato vine (*Ipomoea batatas*), nasturtiums (*Tropaeolum majus*), lobelia (*Lobelia erinus*), wave petunias (*Petunia* x *hybrida*), and trailing begonias (*Begonia solananthera*).

FLOWER POUCHES AND TUBES

An easy and economical way to have bursts of colour hanging on a wall, fence or shed is by using flower tubes

ABOVE *A mixed planting of upright red geraniums and trailing fuchsias creates an attractive hanging display.*

or pouches. These heavy-duty plastic containers come with directions to help you create colourful arrangements that are an eye-catching alternative to the traditional hanging basket. While the casings are not very attractive, they should be hidden once the plants have grown – make sure you choose varieties that will cover them well. The great advantage is that these pouches stretch down and disguise or brighten a much longer vertical length than a basket. You may want to get help hanging them, however, since they are quite heavy once planted up, and make sure you have a stable structure to hang them from. Recommended plants are busy Lizzies (*Impatiens walleriana*), begonias and petunias.

MAINTENANCE

The main care requirement for containers, especially over the summer period, is watering. Any container that is densely planted will need frequent watering, often several times a days in hot sun. Most containers will benefit from regular feeding and deadheading too.

Design focus: vertical planting on walls and fences

Here are three illustrations of vertical planting on existing walls and fences. If your garden is exposed, a well-placed vertical planting, such as a trellis with a climbing clematis, could create privacy or disguise an unattractive feature by increasing the height of an existing wall or fence. Many plants can also be grown over fences or trained on walls. Simple wire grids can also be fastened to the side of a fence to provide guidance for plants that want to seek the heights.

Walls

Solid walls can be used to your advantage in a vertical garden. A lichen-covered stone wall with tiny crevices that are full of mosses or succulents is a thing of beauty and needs no improvement. Other walls of grey cement, breeze (cinder) blocks or new bricks can be dreary and depressing. Shelves can be mounted at various levels on blank walls and these make excellent sites for plant-filled containers.

Fan trellis with clematis (Clematis spp.). Wooden fan or decorative trellises that easily attach to walls provide a stable and showy setting for climbers.

Another option for walls are espalier structures. These work well on a wall that offers a micro-climate of heat and wind protection. With some initial assistance to build the right foundation, you can create a 'two-dimensional' fruit tree that produces healthy and accessible fruit.

Trellises

These gridded and latticed structures are the workhorses of a vertical garden – they can be free-standing or attached to a wall or fence, and many are strong enough to support heavy plants.

Fences

A practical and uninspiring chain-link fence or a rustic split-rail style can be embellished or disguised with plants that like to climb and twirl on their structure.

1 WALL CLIMBERS
Climbing hydrangea (*Hydrangea petiolaris*) and ivy (*Hedera*)

2 ESPALIER PLANTS
Apples (*Malus* spp.), peaches (*Prunus persica*), plums (*Prunus* spp.) and camellia (*see* picture above)

3 TRELLIS PLANTS
Morning glory (*Ipomoea purpurea*), clematis, star jasmine (*Jasminum* spp.), roses, honeysuckle (*Lonicera* spp.), pole beans (*Phaeolus vulgaris*), scarlet runner beans (*Phaseolus coccineus*), peas (*Pisum sativum*), cucumber (*Cucumis sativus*), pumpkins (*Cucurbita* spp.), squash (*Cucurbita* spp.) and grapes (*Vitis vinifera*)

4 FENCING PLANTS
Wisteria, climbing roses, trumpet creeper (*Campsis radicans*), clematis, three-leaf akebia (*Akebia trifoliate*) and passion flower (*Passiflora caerulea*)

Plain trellis with jasmine (Jasminum spp.) and three-leaf akebia (Akebia trifoliata)

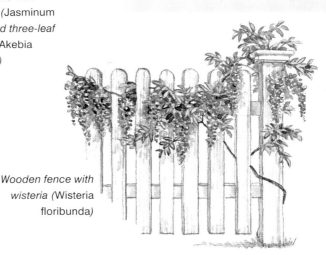

Wooden fence with wisteria (Wisteria floribunda)

Design focus: vertical planting on free-standing structures

Fruit and vegetable gardens have always relied on free-standing vertical structures. These include teepees and obelisks, which look like garden chapel spires with their pointy tips that aim for the heavens and invite sweet-smelling and trailing plants to twist and climb up them. Another free-standing option is a pergola, offering a shady and protective passageway covered with clambering vines and roses that creates a pedestrian connection between a building and the outside world.

Teepees and obelisks

Vegetables benefit from the support offered by teepees and obelisks. Cucumbers will grow straight rather than curved, and beans and peas will hang freely, benefiting from good air circulation and sun exposure. The fruits of squash, melon and pumpkin will need some form of support as they develop to prevent them from breaking off; the small-fruited varieties are best for vertical gardens.

Teepees are fun and easy to make. Bamboo poles, tall willow branches or pliable, recently pruned fruit-tree branches can create attractive and functional tri- or quadri-podded structures for seasonal use. Garden centres also offer a large array of tall, pre-made teepees.

Pergola

The conventional image of a pergola is of a free-standing wooden canopy of crossbeams supported by pillars and covered with climbing vines or roses. It can be any length, depending on the size of your garden.

Arbours and arches

We can be welcomed into a garden by walking under an arched structure covered with leafy, sweet-smelling plants. An arbour goes a step further, inviting us to sit under the shade of the intertwining branches. Fitted with a seat or a bench, this provides a gardener with a place to rest, sip a cool drink and enjoy the view.

1 OBELISK PLANTS

Peas (*Pisum sativum*), climbing beans (*Phaseolus* spp.), butter (lima) beans, cucumbers (*Cucumis melo*), melons, pumpkins, squash, morning glory (*Ipomoea purpurea*) and sweet peas (*Lathyrus odoratus*).

2 PERGOLA PLANTS

Roses (*Rosa* spp.), honeysuckle (*Lonicera* spp.), wisteria (*Wisteria floribunda*), kiwi fruit (*Actinidia deliciosa*) and crimson glory vine (*Vitis coignetiae*).

3 PLANTS FOR ARBOURS AND ARCHES

Clematis, honeysuckle, climbing (not rambling) roses, Chilean glory flower (*Eccremocarpos scaber*), crimson glory vine (*Vitis coignetiae*) and morning glory (*Ipomoea purpurea*).

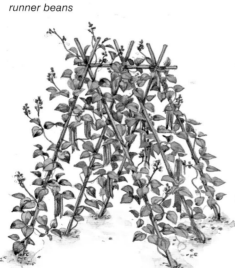

A-frame structure supporting red runner beans

Teepee structure supporting morning glory

Wooden whiskey barrel container planted with nasturtiums

A teepee or trellis in a container allows plants to climb and cascade

Project: planting clematis

Once established, a clematis will give you years of blooms. The best planting time is in the early spring or autumn, during the cooler weather. Unlike most plants, they are best planted more deeply than they were in the pot, to help them recover if they are attacked by clematis wilt. Clematis like their heads in the sun and their feet in the shade. So plant a small shrub or ground cover at its base like evergreen candytuft (Iberis sempervirens) or an evergreen wild strawberry.

ABOVE *You will find a variety of clematis in flower in every season. The flowers head towards the sun as the roots seek the shade.*

MATERIALS

- Support such as trellis or wires attached to a wall or fence, or free-standing
- Spade
- Fork
- Well-composted organic matter/cow manure
- 2 tablespoons of bonemeal
- Clematis plant. *Clematis* 'Etoile Violette' is a reliable and long-term bloomer as well as a variety that is easy to grow and maintain. Other ideas are *C. alpina* 'Candy', with pink blooms in the spring, and *C.* 'Blue Angel', which has gorgeous sky-blue flowers.
- 2–3 small wooden stakes

1 *Dig a 30 x 30cm (12 x 12in) hole 30cm (12in) from the support. Fork in the organic matter and bonemeal.*

2 *Remove the clematis from its pot and tease the roots out gently if they are pot-bound.*

3 *Plant the clematis so it leans towards the support. Bury the plant crown 5cm (2in) below the surface.*

4 *Insert small stakes to act as an initial guide as the plant finds it way to the trellis.*

5 *Water well after planting and then regularly. Use a fertilizer with a low nitrogen content to encourage blossoms and roots.*

Project: planting up a vertical basket

This tiered vertical planter gives you the opportunity to choose and grow an interesting variety of plants and flowers that offer colour contrast, leaf texture and mixed growing habits. The placement and open design gives easy access to all the plants for watering, fertilizing and deadheading. This structure will also add a distinctive design feature to a space that may benefit from an interesting focal point.

ABOVE *Use plants that have similar water and light needs since they will thrive better and be easier to care for.*

MATERIALS

- Tiered structure with fibre baskets
- Mallet or hammer
- Compost (soil mix)
- Young or plugged plants: shown here are *Skimmia japonica*, *Artemisia stelleriana* 'Boughton Silver', Scotch heather (*Calluna vulgaris*), pepper face (*Peperomia obtusifolia* 'Variegata') and dusty miller (*Senecio cineraria*) (top basket); cyclamen (*Cyclamen persicum*), heather, blue fescue (*Festuca glauca*) and *Helichrysum* (middle basket); cyclamen, heather, snow-in-summer (*Cerastium tomentosum*), trailing ivy (*Hedera helix*) and Michaelmas daisy (*Aster* 'Victoria').

1 *Find a good location and securely anchor the legs of the structure into the ground using a mallet or hammer. Assemble the remaining components, making certain that it is sturdy and straight.*

2 *Select a variety of small plants to grow in each basket (see those mentioned in materials list for those used here). Alternatively, you can choose one larger distinctive plant.*

3 *Decide on the combination of plants to fill the pots in each tier. Use a helper so you can stand back to judge the effect.*

4 *Place the selected plants in an empty fibre basket and place this in the wire basket holder.*

5 *Add the compost around the plants and firm them in gently. Water well.*

INDOOR GARDENS

As the weather turns cold, most of us are less keen to spend time in the garden, but we can still keep greenery and living plants around us to animate the interior – and to keep us company. There may also come a time when physical limitations make getting outdoors difficult and inconvenient in any season. Whatever your reasons, creating an indoor garden can improve your quality of life and dramatically boost your emotional and physical well-being.

ABOVE *Forcing hyacinth bulbs indoors during dark winter days brightens up your room and fills the air with sweet fragrance.*

PLANNING AN INDOOR GARDEN

As you would assess your outdoor environment, you also need to survey your indoor space. How much space do you have for plants? How much light do you have and how does it move during the course of the day? Where is your heat source? Are you able to get to the plants easily?

If you are new to keeping plants indoors, start slowly with just one or two. Select the right ones by talking to friends – who may have spare plants as well as advice – and looking in local nurseries. Remember, too, to find out how big the plants may get.

FLOWERS OR FOLIAGE?

Many indoor plants do not flower but are attractive because of the shape and colour of their foliage – examples include pothos, jade (*Crassula ovata*) and begonia. (Rex-cultorum begonias do have attractive flowers, but are mainly grown for their foliage.) If you'd like a flowering plant, try African violets (*Saintpaulia* spp.), cyclamen (*Cyclamen persicum*), and orchids – with the right care these will stay in bloom for many months.

LIGHT LEVELS

Before buying a plant, think carefully about where you will put it because light level requirements vary from plant to plant. Most flowering houseplants need good light levels, but will tolerate a less sunny position for a couple of weeks as long as they are moved back into the light afterwards. Some indoor plants will benefit from being put outside in summer, but they must be acclimatized gradually.

Artificial lighting can help boost light levels indoors, but it can't replace natural daylight. Most houseplants prefer bright, filtered, natural light. This means that they will need a little shade from the hot midday sun. Garden plants are sheltered by other plants and their roots are buried in deep soil, but houseplants are usually alone in a small pot, so the roots easily overheat. Cacti and succulents are happy in full sun, as are some of the geraniums, but you need to watch for scorching because sunshine through glass is very different from sunshine outside.

In general, flowering plants need higher light levels than foliage plants, while plants with large, dark green leaves need less light than those with small, silver-grey leaves. *See* page 111 for more guidance on light levels.

OPPOSITE *To grow roses as successful houseplants, make sure they get full sun for part of the day and don't let the soil dry out.*

BELOW *The begonia family offers many interesting varieties that are versatile and easy to care for.*

ABOVE *The giant taro plant (Alocasia macrorrhiza) can reach 1.2–1.8m (4–6ft) in height.*

TEMPERATURE AND HUMIDITY

Indoor plants come from a wide range of natural habitats, and their needs vary greatly, so it's important to find out what conditions will suit your plants. However, as a general rule, most – apart from cacti and succulents – like a more humid atmosphere than is usually found in centrally heated homes, and in many cases a cooler temperature, especially in winter.

You can raise the humidity around plants by grouping them together, by regular misting, or by standing them on top of a layer of pebbles in a tray filled with water. The latter method is probably the most effective, but the pot should always be above the level of the water.

Houseplants do well in bathrooms and kitchens because of the higher use of water in these rooms. Conservatories (sun rooms) need good ventilation to prevent them overheating. They should be fitted with windows that open, and some form of shading. Opening windows improves air circulation on a warm day, but can also let in cold draughts. Invest in a device with a digital readout, showing inside and outside temperatures, as well as relative humidity.

Signs of inadequate humidity levels are buds falling off or not opening, leaves turning yellow, drooping and turning brown at the tips. In hot weather, mist plants twice a day when there is no direct sun.

WATERING

Giving your plants the correct amount of water is crucial to successful care. Isolating a plant in a pot means that its roots can't search deep down for water,

ABOVE LEFT *Mist the plant foliage once a day with a mister (with the exception of African violets), twice in hot weather.*

LEFT *One watering technique for indoor plants is to water from below, also a good way of rehydrating dry compost.*

as they would in the ground and that water also drains away less quickly.

Spring and summer are the growing seasons for most plants, when they need regular water to produce new growth. They rest in autumn and winter and need just enough water to keep the compost from drying out. Over-watering is the most common cause of death for plants. Except for bog-lovers, they should never be left with the pots standing in water (other than for a few minutes during the watering process).

Many plants dislike hard tap water, especially the lime-haters, such as gardenias. Ideally, use rainwater for these plants, but, if this is difficult, use cooled boiled water or filtered water. The latter is better because it contains no chemical or other soluble salts. If you use tap water, let it sit overnight so that the chlorine evaporates and the water comes to room temperature. When the surface of the compost feels dry, the plant probably needs water. In the dormant period, it's best to dig down a little way with your fingers – it may still be moist enough.

There are several techniques for watering. The first is to water from above using a small, long-spouted watering can, avoiding the leaves and directing the spout at the soil. To make sure the compost gets wet through, water until the saucer at the base is full, and leave to stand for a few minutes. If the water has just run down the sides of the pot, allow it to soak in thoroughly, and then empty the saucer. Alternatively, water from below, allowing the pot to sit in a tray of water until the surface of the compost feels damp. Discard any surplus. This is a good way to rehydrate compost that has become so dry that the water bounces off the top. If the compost has dried out, add a drop of washing-up liquid to the water to allow it to penetrate more easily.

Another technique is to plunge the pot into a bucket of water until the compost is moist, but not waterlogged; then allow the surplus water to drain away.

ABOVE *Liquid feeds offer a balanced mixture of nutrients designed to enhance the characteristics of each plant.*

FEEDING

Fresh compost has added nutrients, but over time these are used up, so potted plants need an occasional feed with a balanced fertilizer.

Liquid feeds are usually sold in concentrated form and need diluting. The feed should be applied when the plant is in growth or flowering. A foliar feed applied to the leaves works as a quick pick-me-up, but move the plants outside before spraying because the minerals in the feed can leave stains.

Other ways of feeding include sprinkling a few slow-release granules into the compost when planting up or pushing a feeding stick into it.

POTTING AND REPOTTING

Plants bought at nurseries and garden centres come in small plastic pots with the roots already trying to escape through the bottom. At some stage they will need to be potted on into a larger pot with fresh compost.

Check all new plants before bringing them indoors. Ease the plant out of its pot and see if there are signs of vine weevil. The plant may show no sign of disease until it flops in the pot and a colony of white grubs with brown heads are found to have attacked the roots.

Plants can be traumatized by being potted on, but will recover most easily if it is done in spring. Use a container that is one or two sizes larger. Cover drainage holes with a coffee filter or piece of fine mesh screen. Add a layer of fresh potting mix and tap down to remove air pockets. Position the plant about 2cm ($^3/_4$in) below the rim to allow for watering. Spoon potting mix around the sides of the rootball and pack it firmly around, pushing down with your thumbs to leave a firm surface.

POTTING COMPOSTS

There are two main types of compost: loam-based and soil-less. Sand or grit can be added to both these mixes to improve drainage.

Loam-based compost is made from sterilized loam with added peat-substitute (or peat) and sand, plus fertilizers in varying amounts; John Innes No.1 contains the least, No. 3 the most. Soil-less composts are traditionally based on peat, but to be kind to the environment use peat substitute versions.

Certain plants need specialist growing mediums. Some orchids and bromeliads, for example, are epiphytic and prefer a loose potting mix that allows air to circulate around them. Cacti and succulents also do better in a free-draining cactus potting mix.

PRUNING

Shaping is probably a better word than pruning to describe the needs of most houseplants, but some vigorous plants do need cutting back.

You can encourage some plants to bush out by pinching out the leading shoots, resulting in new growth down the stem. Begonias and ivies respond well to this type of pruning in spring and summer.

Picking off any flowers that have gone past their best, known as deadheading, encourages the plant to produce more. For example, indoor roses will last much longer if they are deadheaded regularly.

If a plant becomes too large, cut it back using a pair of secateurs (hand pruners). The weeping fig (*Ficus benjamina*) responds well to cutting back quite severely. This is best done in late winter or early spring. Stop climbing plants, such as *Jasminum polyanthum*, becoming straggly by cutting back after flowering and tying in wayward shoots to a framework of canes or wires.

ABOVE *Clean plant leaves every couple of weeks. Wash them with water or use a plant polish and buff with a soft cloth.*

ABOVE *Deadheading encourages the plant to produce more flower buds, and keeps the plant looking good.*

PROPAGATING SEMI-SUCCULENTS

Plants are programmed to propagate themselves. As well as producing seeds, many plants have evolved so that a leaf or piece of stem that is accidentally broken off will root and form a new plant if it lands in a favourable spot. Gardeners take advantage of this phenomenon by taking cuttings, using a variety of techniques to give the plants ideal conditions for taking root. The best times are in spring and summer when there is plenty of light and warmth. The larger, fleshier leaves of some succulents, such as echeverias, crassulas and begonias, can be used to form new plants. There are various methods – this technique shows how to propagate from an individual begonia leaf using perlite.

1 *Select a young healthy leaf. Cut it at the plant base and then cut leaving a short stem.*

2 *Using a scalpel, make a 1cm (½in) incision straight across each of the strongest veins.*

3 *Using thin wire bent into a 'U' shape, pin down the leaf on a tray of damp cutting compost.*

4 *Each vein should produce roots. When plantlets develop, separate them and pot them on.*

CARING FOR AFRICAN VIOLETS

African violets (*Saintpaulia* spp.) have a reputation for being tricky to keep healthy. This is not necessarily true, but they do like plenty of light, and they dislike draughts and changes in temperature. If you work around these preferences they should respond well. A reassuring tip is that African violets seem to do best when their roots are tightly confined.

1 *Find a location for your African violet that has bright but not direct sunlight. Make sure the pot is sitting in a tray that can be used for watering.*

2 *Fill the tray with pebbles. Add a moderate amount of water to the tray. The surface soil must dry out between watering. Do not get water on the leaves.*

3 *Each week turn the plant on a half rotation so that all sides get equal light.*

4 *Apply African violet fertilizer every 2–3 weeks to maintain healthy foliage and encourage repeat flowering.*

Design focus: plants and quality of light

All plants need adequate light to thrive. Fortunately, we have choices – some plants like a low light (north-facing windows in the Northern Hemisphere or south-facing windows in the Southern Hemisphere); some need as much light as they can get (south-facing windows in the Northern Hemisphere or north-facing in the Southern Hemisphere). Some plants prefer a more gentle, indirect light, suitable for an east or west-facing window. Here are some of plants that thrive in these light conditions.

PLANTS THAT SUIT A FULL WARM LIGHT

A warm and sunny exposure suits succulents, cacti and bromeliads. The strength of the sun will depend on the latitude, time of year and the orientation of the room.

PLANTS THAT SUIT A COLD, LOW LIGHT

These plants are undemanding in that they do not want to be over-heated, over-watered or overfed. Give them regular mistings of water to create humidity in the air.

PLANTS THAT SUIT A PARTIAL LIGHT

Turn these plants by a third of a rotation every week or two so they grow evenly.

FULL-SUN PLANTS

1. Herbs (basil, oregano, parsley, rosemary)
2. Jade plant (*Crassula arborescens*)
3. Agave (*Agave americana*)
4. Medicine plant (*Aloe vera*)
5. Chives (*Allium schoenoprasum*)
6. Bromeliad (*Bromeliad* spp.)
7. Sage (*Salvia officinalis*)

PARTIAL-LIGHT PLANTS

8. Orchid (various species)
9. Spider plant (*Chlorophytum comosum*)
10. and **11** Begonia (*Begonia* spp.) (*see* picture above)
12. Prayer plant (*Maranta leucoreura*)
13. Swedish ivy (*Plectranthus australis*)
14. Grape ivy (*Cissus rhombifolia*)
15. African violets (*Saintpaulia* spp.)
16. Japanese aralia (*Fatsia japonica*)

LOW-LIGHT PLANTS

17. Philodendron (*Philodendron*)
18. Cast iron plant (*Aspidistra elatior*)
19. Peace lily (*Spathiphyllum*)
20. Chinese evergreen (*Aglaonema commutatum*)
21. Snake plant/mother in law's tongue (*Sansevieria trifasciata*)

PLANT DIRECTORY

Compiling a plant directory such as this is a bit like being a child in a candy store – there are just so many choices! Because of space limitations not all the wonderful and appropriate plants, trees, shrubs and edibles can be included. But by visiting local nurseries, reading garden magazines and books, joining a garden group, and, if you're so inclined, surfing the internet, you can discover many more interesting plants that will keep your mind and hands busy gardening.

The selections shown here are designed both for ease of maintenance and breadth of appeal. The directory is also meant to be easy to read and to provide necessary information to make good plant choices. This listing is intended to help, encourage and motivate experienced gardeners who may need some additional guidance as they age, maybe moving to a new residence with an unfamiliar garden or learning to live with a physical limitation that affects what is possible for them to do as gardeners. It is also for seniors who are new to gardening – it is never too late to begin learning!

OPPOSITE *Fill your garden space with annuals and perennials, flowers that will keep you company throughout the season.*

ABOVE *Keep the names of your plants documented by using plant labels, useful if you want to check care requirements.*

ABOVE *A selection of herbs, including fennel, sage, hyssop and oregano, grows in a walled garden bed.*

ABOVE *Smaller sized dahlias will bloom earlier and rebloom more quickly, rewarding you with more flowers.*

THE CLASSIFICATION AND NAMING OF PLANTS

The 18th-century botanist Carl Linnaeus devised a system for classifying all living things. He gave plants two Latinized names to show their relationship to all other living things. A plant genus, the first of the two, is a group of plants containing similar species. A species, the second of the two, refers to a group of individuals capable of breeding with each other.

ABOVE Thunbergia alata, *a perky and petite annual vine, loves the sun and provides red, pink, orange and bright yellow blooms.*

SCIENTIFIC NAMES

A plant's botanical, scientific or Latin name, though often derived from Latin, frequently contains Greek and other languages. Some genera contain species that may include annuals, perennials, shrubs and trees, and these may look different from one another even though they are related. Others might contain just one species or a group of species that bear obvious similarities.

A species is defined as consisting of individuals that are alike and tend naturally to breed with each other. Despite this definition, botanists and taxonomists (the experts who classify living things) often disagree about the basis on which a plant has been named. As the science continues to be refined, more old inaccuracies are coming to the fore. Having old names in common usage creates confusion, and plant names often include the old name or synonym (syn. for short) after the correct name. Understandably, gardeners often become frustrated with the seemingly

BELOW *A collection of smaller containers kept on a garden table can be maintained easily, without bending or physical strain.*

constant name changing, but it is useful to keep abreast of them. Update your library with a good, recently published pocket reference book and take it with you when you shop for plants.

VARIATIONS ON A THEME

In the average garden, you may grow a single species that is represented by small but pleasing differences such as variegated leaves, differently coloured or double flowers. The terms for these variations are subspecies (subsp.), variety (var.), form (f.) – similar to variety and often used interchangeably – and cultivar (cv.). A cultivar is a variation that has been selected or artificially bred and is maintained by cultivation. Cultivars are given names in single quotation marks. So, a cultivar of the Japanese apricot is *Prunus mume* 'Beni Chidori'.

HYBRIDS AND GROUPS

When plant species breed with each other, the result is a hybrid. While rare in the wild, crossing is common among plant breeders and is done to produce plants with desirable qualities such as larger or double blooms, longer flowering time or greater frost resistance. A multiplication sign (x) is used to indicate a hybrid and the name often gives a clear idea of its origins.

A group is a cluster of plants with variations that are so similar they cannot be separated. Their names do not have quotation marks (for example, Andersoniana Group).

HOW TO USE
THE DIRECTORY

The first category in the directory, on container plants, is designed for those with limited energy and space. The following four categories give examples of plants and then trees that thrive in sun or shade. The next three categories show easy-to-grow edible crops – vegetables, fruit and herbs. Finally, a category on indoor plants suits those with no garden or who prefer to garden inside. A typical entry is shown below, with explanations of the component elements.

ABOVE Salvia farinacea 'Victoria Blue' (mealy sage) has deep blue flowers and combines well with other perennials.

Genus and species name

The first part of this internationally accepted botanical name, the genus, denotes a group of related plant species (or sometimes a single species); the second part defines a specific species. It may be further defined by a subspecies, hybrid, variant or cultivar name. Sometimes a synonym (syn.) is also given.

Family name

This shows the larger grouping to which the plant belongs. Knowing the plant's family name will sometimes indicate which plants are susceptible to the same diseases.

Cultivation

These notes give a brief recipe as to the best conditions in which to grow the plant, such as the level of sun or shade that the plant either requires or tolerates, with advice on the best type of soil in which it should be grown.

Notes

This section provides relevant and interesting information about the sensory aspects of a plant, its value for crafts or other uses, or a particular cultivar or variety that should be considered. Other information may include details of hybrids (indicated by an 'x' in the name) and recommended varieties and cultivars (featuring names in single quotations) that are available.

Caption

A full or shortened botanical name is given with each photograph.

Photograph

A large number of entries feature a full-colour photograph, which makes identification easier.

- *Foeniculum vulgare*
  FENNEL
- **FAMILY** Apiaceae
  This handsome perennial will add grace, height and texture. With bright green, finely fern-like leaves and aromatic yellow flowers, it's best planted in the back of the herb or perennial flower garden as it will grow to 90–120cm (3–4ft).
- **CULTIVATION** The plants require full sunlight and well-drained, deep, moderately fertile soil. Best planted in a more spacious garden where architectural structure may be needed.
  HARDINESS Fully hardy/Z5
- **NOTES** Fennel attracts bees, butterflies and birds. All parts of the plant are edible – the leaves, stems, seeds and roots. The plants release a chemical that inhibits the growth of some other plants, so do not plant very close to beans, tomatoes or cabbage family plants.
  MAINTENANCE Easy. It seeds freely so new seedlings will require weeding to control their spread.

- BELOW Foeniculum vulgare

Common name

This is the popular, non-scientific name. It may apply to the whole or part of the plant genus. There are sometimes a variety of common names.

Genus description

Describes what the plant looks like at different times of year and its popularity. Includes a description of the leaves and, when applicable, the flowers and fruits. The expected height and sometimes spread of a genus or individual plant are often given, although growth rates vary depending on location. Metric always precede imperial measurements. The dimensions of bulbs, annuals and perennials tend to be more consistent than those of shrubs, long-lived climbers and trees.

Hardiness

Each plant's hardiness and zone are given, with the exception of vegetables and indoor plants. The categories are fully hardy, frost hardy, half hardy and frost tender for the UK and Europe, and USDA zones are given for the USA. The hardiness zones give a general indication of the average annual minimum temperature for a particular geographical area. The small number indicates the northernmost zone it can survive in and the higher number the southernmost zone that the plant will tolerate. In most cases, only one zone is given. (*See also* page 160 for details of hardiness definitions, zone entries and a zone map.)

Maintenance

Indicates whether low or moderate care is needed (intensive-care options are not given). Suggestions are often included, and additional information on plant care.

CONTAINER PLANTS

Many elders feel that their gardening days are over when they leave the family home with its in-ground beds, trees and a lawn to tend. However, a smaller garden filled with container plants has options on a different scale, including small, decorative herb-filled pots on a windowsill, large wooden tubs of blueberry bushes and mixed displays of bedding plants outside your back door that bring scintillating colours and perfume to your garden. Even if you no longer have a garden at all, you can grow a surprising range of plants in large window boxes and hanging baskets.

ABOVE *A selection of annuals in a terracotta pot, including* Cordyline australis *in the centre.*

Calibrachoa x *hybrida*
MINI PETUNIA, MILLION BELLS SERIES
FAMILY Solanaceae

This tender perennial produces flowers that look like small petunias. Perfect for containers, they are compact, mounded plants growing 7.5–23cm (3–9in) tall on mostly trailing stems. Prolific bloomers, they produce hundreds of 2.5cm (1in) width flowers from spring through to the first frost. Flower colours include shades of violet, blue, pink, red, magenta, yellow, bronze and white.

BELOW Calibrachoa *'Sunbelfire', Million Bells Series*.

CULTIVATION Grow in light, well-drained compost in full sun. Mini petunias can tolerate very light shade, but flowering will decrease as the shade increases. It dislikes very wet soil, and tolerates drought – in fact it's best to let it dry out between waterings to guard against fungal disease. Set plants out after the last frost.
HARDINESS Frost hardy/Z9–11
NOTES Choose from many hybrids that provide a rainbow of colours as you design your containers and hanging baskets. *Calibrachoa* is a hummingbird attractor.
MAINTENANCE Easy. Self-cleaning, no deadheading necessary. It is susceptible to aphids, but they can be washed off with a jet of water.

Chamaecyparis obtusa 'Pygmaea'
HINOKI FALSE CYPRESS
FAMILY Cupressaceae

This important landscape conifer provides a garden with a graceful slender upright tree with attractive orange-brown stems and nodding branch tips. It reaches a height of only 1.5m (5ft), although it grows much larger in its native Japan. The twisted, deep-green branchlets are held on tiered branches, creating an open habit.
CULTIVATION Dwarf hinoki cypress thrives in well-drained, humus-rich soil in bright shade. If grown in full sun, give careful attention to watering during the summer. It is drought-tolerant in part shade. In hot climates provide protection from the hot afternoon sun.
HARDINESS Fully hardy/Z4–8
NOTES There are many other 'dwarf' cultivars, but most of them are too big for a container.
MAINTENANCE Easy. Protect from the wind. This small tree can be shaped to accommodate tight quarters.

Cordyline australis 'Charlie Boy'
CORDYLINE
FAMILY Agavaceae

Often grown indoors, cordyline is finding a prominent place in stunning annual container gardens, as well as in borders. Providing height, colour and texture with spiky upright leaves, it adds contrast to the bushy and cascading colourful annuals that it shares space with. 'Charlie Boy' has variegated leaves with a burgundy central stripe and bright pink margins and reaches a height of 2m (7ft).
CULTIVATION Plant in a sunny spot in well-drained compost in a container that can be moved. Initial shelter will be needed as it gets established.
HARDINESS Half hardy/Z10
NOTES Suitable for growing indoors.
MAINTENANCE Easy. Dislikes waterlogged soil and temperatures below 8°C (17°F). Move to a sheltered area or wrap in fleece or hessian (burlap) if temperatures drop.

Imperata cylindrica rubra 'Red Baron'
JAPANESE BLOOD GRASS
FAMILY **Poaceae**

This perennial, non-invasive, slow-spreading grass is a striking accent in a container because of its spectacular green, red-tipped foliage. It forms an upright clump about 50cm (20in) tall and wide. As the seasons age into the autumn the blades become redder and finally turn to a dark red maroon. It is a wonderful complement to blue and purple flowers or lovely just as a mass planting in a large container.

BELOW Ipomoea batatas *'Margarita'*.

CULTIVATION This plant loves full sun and prefers being in a well-drained container. In hotter climates it will appreciate light shade. While it is fairly drought-tolerant, don't allow it to dry out during prolonged dry spells, which will cause the tips to brown.

HARDINESS Half hardy/Z5–9

NOTES If possible, position the container of 'Red Baron' blood grass where the morning or late afternoon sun can backlight the leaves, giving off a dramatic red colour glow.

MAINTENANCE Easy. After the blades turn to a straw colour in the winter, cut the plant to the ground.

ABOVE I. cylindrica rubra *'Red Baron'*.

Ipomoea batatas 'Margarita'
SWEET POTATO VINE
FAMILY **Convolvulaceae**

This 'potato' is grown for its fan-shaped leaves that are a bright chartreuse colour. It will trail attractively over the edge of a container. 'Margarita' accents plants with darker foliage. It reaches a height of 10–25cm (4–10in).

CULTIVATION These plants grow best in a sunny location with relatively warm temperatures. Plant in a good, light, well-drained soil. Once established, the sweet potato vine is not particularly thirsty, since the underground tuber retains enough water to get through some dry spells.

HARDINESS Half hardy to frost tender/Z9–11

NOTES 'Blackie' is a variety with dark purple, nearly black foliage and 'Tricolour' has pale green, white and pink margined leaves. Mix these in a container for a lovely show.

MAINTENANCE Easy. Prune often if needed to control for size and to create more branching. It can be kept over winter if the container is protected from frost.

Lobelia erinus
LOBELIA
FAMILY **Campanulaceae**

Lobelia is a perennial usually grown as an annual for summer bedding and containers. There are trailing varieties, with billowing masses of blossoms, and more compact bedding which seldom exceeds 15cm (6in) in height. The 1–2cm (½–¾in) wide flowers that grow along each stem come in blue, white and carmine.

CULTIVATION Lobelia does best in full sun and in moist, rich soil where summers are cool. It will grow well in hot areas if given partial shade and ample water. Plant out after all danger of frost is past, spacing the plants 10–15cm (4–6in) apart if in the ground.

HARDINESS Half hardy/Z10–11

NOTES A perfect plant for window boxes, hanging baskets, planters, groundcover or border edgings, as it gives a softness of colour and texture. Look for the colour varieties – especially beautiful are the blue palates of 'Cambridge Blue' or the lavender shades of 'Riviera' – and match them with yellows and oranges to create a stunning feast of colour.

MAINTENANCE Easy. Lobelia has virtually no disease or pest problems. Shear the flower spikes after blooming to promote further growth.

Lobularia maritima
SWEET ALYSSUM
FAMILY **Brassicaceae**

Also known as Carpet of Snow, this fragrant favourite – an annual or short-lived perennial – produces masses of crisp white blooms. Perfect for window boxes and other containers, it grows only 10cm (4in) tall, so works well hugging the outer edges of pots. Ideal for ground cover, too, as its growth is wide spreading and it flowers all summer.

CULTIVATION Grow in full sun to partial shade. Does well in well-drained, light soil.

HARDINESS Fully hardy/5–9

NOTES This sturdy plant adorns coastal gardens as it tolerates wind and salt spray. It attracts butterflies and bees. Alice Series and Easter Bonnet Series cultivars are compact and have flower in white, rose-pink and purple-pink.

BELOW Lobelia erinus.

ABOVE Lobularia maritima.

MAINTENANCE Easy. After first flowering, cut back to enjoy another wave of blooms.

Laurus nobilis
SWEET BAY
FAMILY **Lauraceae**

This small, evergreen tree is a slow grower. Its height range is 3.6–12m (12–40ft). Its attractive 7.5cm (3in) leathery leaves are long, deep-green, pointed and deliciously fragrant. The small yellow flowers come in umbel clusters that appear over two months in the early summer.

CULTIVATION Likes well-drained, sandy soil with some moisture. Grow in a sunny spot in pots with good drainage. Allow to dry slightly between waterings.

HARDINESS Frost hardy/Z8–10

NOTES The dried leaves are a wonderful addition to soups and stews.

MAINTENANCE Easy. Ensure you can move the container to shelter if temperatures drop below 2°C (28°F).

Lysimachia nummularia 'Aurea'
CREEPING JENNY, MONEYWORT
FAMILY **Primulaceae**

This vigorous yellow-lime-green leafy creeper is best limited to containers since it has the ability to take over beds

ABOVE *Lysimachia nummularia* 'Aurea'.

A light mulch will cool the roots. They perform well in combination warm, dry days and cool evenings and bloom best when the roots are a little pot bound. Water regularly.

HARDINESS Frost tender/Z9–10
NOTES Another geranium variety includes the 'Martha Washington', with heart-shaped leaves with crinkled edges and showy flowers. This is widely recognized as a first-class potted plant.
MAINTENANCE Easy. Deadhead the spent flowers to encourage continuous bloom. In cold climates they can be brought indoors as a houseplant.

ABOVE *P. x hortorum* '*Mrs Pollock*'.

and pathways. Managing it in containers will add fabulous colour contrasts and textures to your arrangement. Prolific, cup-shaped, bright yellow flowers (with a diameter of less than 2.5cm/1in) appear in early summer.
CULTIVATION Grow in good potting soil in full sun in a cool climate, or in shade in a warm climate. The yellow hue shows in full sun, while foliage is lime green in shade. Prefers moist soils. Intolerant of dry soils.
HARDINESS Fully hardy/Z4–8
NOTES This plant is mainly grown for its foliage and the way it spills over containers and hanging baskets.
MAINTENANCE Easy.

Pelargonium x *hortorum* 'Mrs. Pollock'
GERANIUM
FAMILY Geraniaceae
This annual, while common in name, offers bold-textured clusters of floral heads from white, pink, red, salmon, orange and violet. Add to this the lush, medium to dark green foliage that has bronze zonal bands and you have an uncommon, reliable and long-blooming container plant.
CULTIVATION Grow these in full sun to partial sun in moist, well-drained soil.

RIGHT Petunia *x* hybrida *Surfinia Series*

Petunia x *hybrida*
PETUNIA
FAMILY Solanaceae
A popular annual that easily adds a wide range of bloom colour to baskets and containers. Thick and sticky broad green leaves accent the funnel-shaped or heavily ruffled blooms. Colours include deep or pale pink, yellow, red, purple and white. Of the many cultivars, the Surfinia Series are especially suitable for hanging baskets, as they can trail down for as much as 90cm (3ft), with large, showy flowers and bushy growth.
CULTIVATION Plant in full sun using a light, well-drained compost. Like regular water and monthly feeding with a complete fertilizer. Heavy rains spoil blooms so if possible, move petunia containers to a sheltered area.
HARDINESS Half hardy/Z10–11
NOTES For small containers or the edging of boxes and planters, choose rosy 'Bright Eyes' with a white throat, rose-starred white 'Twinkle's, light 'Silvery Blue' and white 'Igloo'. The Surfinia Series cultivars have some resistance to rain damage.
MAINTENANCE Easy. Pinch tips to encourage branching, and keep bushy and compact. Remove faded blooms twice a week to improve appearance and encourage repeat flowering.

Salvia farinacea 'Victoria Blue'
SALVIA
FAMILY Lamiaceae

Saliva, or flowering sage, has graced gardens for many years. Over 900 species are available worldwide, so the choice of the attractive 'Victoria Blue' saves you researching all the options. This perennial grows 45–60cm (18–24in) tall, and has intense violet-blue flowers that are densely packed along the stalk. Salvia blooms all summer long. The grey-green foliage is also attractive.

CULTIVATION Salvias like a light, well-drained compost and full sun. In very hot climates, light shade is fine. Give moderate amounts of water to young plants but once established this salvia is able to thrive with low moisture.

HARDINESS Half hardy/Z8–10

NOTES This plant attracts bees, butterflies and other desirable insects and discourages less desirable ones. It can be used in cut-flower arrangements or dried for a longer-lasting display.

MAINTENANCE Easy. Deadheading spent flowers will keep the plant blooming and looking good.

Tagetes erecta
AFRICAN MARIGOLD
FAMILY Compositae

Common African marigold varieties are strong in the orange and yellow colour range, but they also include lovely maroon, red and creamy white shades. Plant heights can vary from 15–90cm (6in–3ft) with flowers from tiny, 1cm (½in) singles to huge, 10–13cm (4–5in) doubles. Marigold leaves are a rich dark green and are finely cut and fernlike.

CULTIVATION Marigold plants are annuals, and are easy to grow from seed. They prefer full to partial sun as well as rich well-drained soil that is not wet. They are very tolerant of average to slightly poor soils and

although they prefer regular watering, they will survive dry periods.

HARDINESS Half hardy/Z8–10

NOTES The related but generally more compact French marigolds (*Tagetes patula*) are often grown as a companion plant, as their strong aroma deters many insect pests. They like similar conditions to their cousins, but the flowers are less susceptible to rain damage than the larger, more frilly African ones. French marigolds offer a much broader colour range, including rich reds, mahogany and bi-colours. Most marigolds are hybrids, so if you save seed from last year's plants, they may not be the same as the originals.

MAINTENANCE Easy. Add a general-purpose fertilizer once a month. Slugs can do major damage, so use an organic slug deterrent or barrier to keep them away.

Tropaeolum majus
NASTURTIUM
FAMILY Tropaeolaceae

A reliable old garden favourite, the trailing nasturtium is an annual that will adorn a container with bright green round leaves surrounded by funnel-shaped flowers in red, orange, maroon and yellow-cream.

ABOVE Tagetes erecta *Jubilee Series*.

CULTIVATION They do best in full sun, in a poor, well-drained compost. Over-fertilizing will promote more leafy growth at the expense of flowers.

HARDINESS Fully hardy to frost tender/Z10–11

NOTES Use as a cut flower or use the young leaves and flowers in salads. 'Peach Melba' is a good choice for containers.

MAINTENANCE Easy. Pick the flowers to encourage further flowering. Aphids like these, but a stream of water from the hose can wash them away easily.

BELOW Tropaeolum majus.

FLOWERS AND PLANTS THAT PREFER FULL SUN

In regions that have hot dry summers or gardens with areas that are sizzling sun traps, you will need a set of plants that will thrive as the temperature climbs and will not create unreasonable demands for watering. Many plants like plenty of light, but a large proportion are content either in full sun or partial shade. Here you will find some that will only thrive well in full sun, and others that are happy with one or the other, or a mixture. Another approach is to concentrate on sun-loving plants native to your region – these will have the best chance of success.

ABOVE Coreopsis verticillata, *the thread-leaf coreopsis, has delicate yellow flowers in loose, open clusters on thin, wiry stems.*

LEFT Allium *x* hollandicum.

Achillea millefolium
YARROW
FAMILY Asteraceae

Yarrow produces flattened clusters of red, pink or white flowers on slender stems clad in feathery green foliage. Plants will typically reach a height of around 60cm (2ft).

CULTIVATION Grow in full sun and well-drained soil. Yarrow is drought-tolerant once it is established. Dividing every other year promotes air circulation, thereby cutting down on problems with powdery mildew.

HARDINESS Fully hardy/Z3–8

NOTES These summer flowers are great for fresh or dried arrangements. Yarrow may suffer from aphids, but also attracts many other insects including ladybirds and parasitic wasps, both of which prey on aphids.

MAINTENANCE Moderate. Yarrow plants should be staked since they do flop down on the ground after high winds. Trimming the plants back after flowering will encourage new blooms.

Allium
ALLIUM
FAMILY Liliaceae

Round heads of alliums floating above mounds of foliage are a magical sight. Leave the seedheads as long as you can as they create a good structure for the planting. Provides nectar for bees and other insects. Height varies with variety.

CULTIVATION Alliums like well-drained soil in a sunny location. Plant bulbs 15cm (6in) deep.

HARDINESS Fully hardy/Z6–10

NOTES 'Firmament' and 'Purple Sensation' are robust and long-lasting. For maximum impact, plant bulbs of *A. giganteum* throughout herbaceous or mixed borders.

MAINTENANCE Easy.

Aquilegia
COLUMBINE
FAMILY **Ranunculaceae**

Columbines are delicately poised garden perennials that grow 38–50cm (15–20in). They produce large, showy blooms of single and bicolour patterns on airy plants with blue-green foliage. The blooms appear from late spring to early summer. Colours include shades of yellow, white, pink, blue, purple and combinations. Add this plant to any garden for years of dependable flowers.

CULTIVATION These grow well in full or partial shade and in average soils that drain well. These plants tolerate dry soil conditions. Once your columbines are established, they will grow well and bloom until the first frost.

HARDINESS Fully to frost hardy/Z4–9

NOTES Columbine is a favourite of both hummingbirds and bees because the flowers contain lots of nectar. A versatile plant, it does well in flowerbeds, containers, as an edging plant and especially in rock gardens.

MAINTENANCE Easy. They self-seed but are not invasive. They don't require mulching or protection in the winter. In mid-season if they look shabby, prune to the ground and you may get a late autumn bloom.

BELOW Aster novi-belgii.

ABOVE Aquilegia canadensis.

Aster novi-belgii
MICHAELMAS DAISY
FAMILY **Asteraceae**

This aster blooms just as the other summer flowers fade. Its bright and prolific plants produce large clusters of delicate daisy-like flowers in white, purple, lavender, pink or red, from late summer to late autumn. Some grow less than 30cm (1ft) tall, while others are 60cm (2ft) tall or more.

CULTIVATION Asters are happiest when planted in moist well-drained soil but they adapt to most soil types. They love to be in full sun, but will tolerate light shading.

HARDINESS Fully hardy/Z4–8

NOTES Asters are one of the largest families of flowering plants, so enjoy finding the best variety for your garden space. Michaelmas daisies are hybrids of *A. novi-belgii* and *A. novae-angliae*. They are called Michaelmas daisies because they bloom around Michaelmas, or St Michael's Day (29 September).

MAINTENANCE Moderate. Pinch back the tops by 15–20cm (6–8in) around midsummer in order to create a bushier plant and to prolong the autumn bloom. Divide the plant every two to three years by simply digging out half to two-thirds of the plants and leave the remainder in place. Share the divisions with a neighbour!

Briza maxima
QUAKING GRASS
FAMILY **Poaceae**

This ornamental plant is a graceful and delicate grass that gives elegance to a garden bed or dried flower arrangements. It grows to 30–60cm (1–2ft) high with thin 15cm (6in) leaves. Bunches of straw-coloured nodding seed heads that resemble rattlesnake rattles dangle from the thin stems.

CULTIVATION Quaking grass likes full sun and will be happy in any well-drained soil with minimal water needs.

HARDINESS Fully hardy/Z5–9

NOTES Gather when the heads have changed colour but before they start to break up, and hang them in bunches, heads down, in a cool, dry airy place. Spray with silver and gold to add sparkle to winter arrangements.

MAINTENANCE Easy. May self-seed but new seedlings are easy to control.

Clematis 'Niobe'
CLEMATIS
FAMILY **Ranunculaceae**

This climbing vine is perfect for small spaces and accessible trellises and grows to a height of 2–3m (7–10ft). The lovely velvety, burgundy, single flowers are 10–15cm (4–6in) in diameter with bright yellow anthers at their centres. These stunning blooms will grace your garden all summer, and the fluffy, spiral-shaped seed heads will then stay on for months.

CULTIVATION This plant is easily grown in fertile, medium-moisture, well-drained soil in full sun to part shade. It should be planted 5–7.5cm (2–3in) deeper than it was in the pot, so that if it is attacked by clematis wilt, it will have a good chance of recovery. Clematis in general like their 'feet in the shade and heads in the sun'. Planting a small evergreen bush or dense ground cover around the base will give the roots the shade and coolness they need. Always add thick mulch around the plant in late winter for a good spring growth spurt.

BELOW Clematis *'Niobe'*.

HARDINESS Frost hardy/Z4–9

NOTES There are many different types of clematis, and by growing several you can have flowers from early spring to late autumn. The vigorous *C. montana* will cover a large wall or fence with pale pink or white flowers in spring. Clematis are also lovely when grown through a tree or a large rambler rose – make sure you match the size of the host plant to the potential size of the clematis.

MAINTENANCE Moderate. Feed rose food weekly just before flowering. Because its bloom is mostly from the current year's stems, cut back stems hard in late winter or early spring before new growth appears. (Note that the different types of clematis require different pruning regimes.)

Coreopsis verticillata 'Moonbeam'
MOONBEAM COREOPSIS, TICKSEED
FAMILY **Asteraceae**

A graceful perennial that grows erect stems 45–61cm (1½–2ft) high and about 45cm (1⅛ft) wide. Its airy foliage forms whorls of finely divided narrow leaves, culminating with pale yellow daisy-like blossoms on the tips of the stems. The plant dances in the breeze.

CULTIVATION Make sure you have a very sunny spot in well-drained soil for the 'Moonbeam', which likes a dry to medium moisture. Hardy and tough, it can thrive in poor, sandy or rocky soils with good drainage. Tolerant of heat, humidity and drought.

HARDINESS Fully hardy/Z6

NOTES 'Moonbeam' is a sterile cultivar, so does not reseed but does spread by rhizomes. A big attraction to bees and butterflies, it also brings birds (especially finches) if you leave the seed heads on.

MAINTENANCE: Easy. For a second bloom, wait until the first flush of flowers wane and then shear the entire plant back. Recovery will be quick, although prompt deadheading of flower stalks can be tedious for a large planting.

ABOVE Crocosmia *'Lucifer'*.

Crocosmia 'Lucifer'
MONTBRETIA
FAMILY **Iridaceae**

This dramatic perennial plant features tubular, nodding, scarlet flowers that bloom on the upper portions of stiffly arching stems. Narrow, sword-shaped leaves rise above a basal clump and salute the other flowers and shimmy in the breeze. A tall grower, it can reach 90cm–1.2m (3–4ft).

CULTIVATION Grown from corms, montbretia likes average to medium moisture, well-drained soil in full sun to part shade. It prefers moist soils if grown in full sun but it is tolerant of summer heat and humidity.

HARDINESS Half hardy/Z5–9

NOTES This old-time favourite is a good cut flower and an eye-catching garden specimen. Hummingbirds are attracted to the colour and the trumpet-shaped flowers. Some other attractive varieties (not 'Lucifer') can be invasive, so plant the corms in a large, bottomless pot or bucket buried in the ground. This way you have that wonderful blast of colour but the plants are controlled.

MAINTENANCE Easy. Watch for spider mites and thrips. In colder regions, the corms can be stored like gladioli, wintered in pots, or mulched heavily outdoors.

Dahlia
DAHLIA
FAMILY **Asteraceae**

A great plant for adding bold splashes of colour to the garden, dahlias will flower prolifically from midsummer to the first frosts, making them especially welcome when many other plants are past their best. The flowerheads – in many forms from daisy-like to pom-pom-like – can be as small as 5cm (2in) or up to 30cm (1ft) in diameter and in all colours apart from blue. Heights range from 30cm (1ft) to 1.8–2.5m (6–8ft).

CULTIVATION Dahlias need soil warmth to be 14.5–15.5°C (58–60°F). Very wet soil may cause the tubers to rot, so wait for a drying trend when the soil is moist but not soggy. Dig and prepare the planting hole depending on growth size of the tuber. Mix a spadeful of compost, a handful of bonemeal, and a little lime into the soil. For taller varieties, put in a stake when planting (doing it later could damage the tuber).

HARDINESS Half hardy/Z7–10

NOTES 'Alva's Doris' is a warm season, tender perennial with small,

BELOW Echinacea purpurea.

ABOVE Dahlia *'Kay Helen'*.

doubled, semi-cactus flowers in a brilliant red; 'Mary Richards' is a small-flowered dahlia with white flowers and a lavender-pink sheen; 'Fascination' has pinkish-purple flowers and dark bronze foliage; 'Hillcreat Ultra' is a decorative dahlia with small flowers with pink outer petals and lemon-yellow inner petals.

MAINTENANCE Moderate. Deadhead regularly to encourage long flowering. When autumn frosts begin, cut them down to 15cm (6in), dig up the tubers and store, frost-free, in dry sand or peat substitute over winter.

Echinacea purpurea
CONEFLOWER
FAMILY **Asteraceae**

This perennial flowering plant grows smooth, 60cm–1.5m (2–5ft) stems that support flowers of domed, purplish-brown, hard spiny centres and drooping lavender rays. Bristly oblong leaves grow smaller near the top of the stem. Blooming begins in late spring or early summer. In the autumn, leave the faded flowers in place and watch how the spiky seed heads feed the finches.

CULTIVATION Prefers a deep rich loam and a sunny position. Coneflowers thrive in either dry or moist soil and can tolerate drought once they are established.

HARDINESS Fully hardy/Z4–9

NOTES Some varieties of *Echinacea* are used for medicinal purposes, mainly to boost the immune system, but *E. purpurea* is not one that is used as a herbal remedy. It should only be used as an ornamental perennial.

MAINTENANCE Easy. A robust and sturdy plant that seldom needs staking, and gives a garden several seasons of interest.

Eupatorium purpureum
JOE-PYE WEED
FAMILY **Asteraceae**

Conveniently, Joe-Pye blooms later in the summer when the garden is in need of a boost. Tall sturdy stalks rise like a fountain from a multi-stemmed clump, and then present glorious clusters of rosy pink to light purple flowers. Stems in bloom reach 2.2m (7ft) tall.

CULTIVATION Grow in full sun to partial shade in a moist, rich soil. In the heat, they need regular watering. Plants are slow to emerge in spring, so place markers by the clumps.

HARDINESS Fully hardy/Z4–9

NOTES The flowers attract butterflies as well as a great many other garden visitors. The added bonus of Joe-Pye weed is the subtle vanilla scent of the leaves. Consider using the variety 'Atropurpureum', which has deep purple stems, and the white-flowered 'Album' variety.

MAINTENANCE Moderate. For shorter plants and more blooms, cut stems back by half in early summer.

Hemerocallis 'Stella de Oro'
DAYLILY
FAMILY **Liliaceae**

One of the finest dwarf daylilies with its repeating masses of bright, golden-yellow, trumpet-shaped, fragrant flowers in early summer. They reach 30cm (1ft) tall and wide. You can't go wrong if you have several daylilies in your garden beds.

CULTIVATION It prefers full sun and moist, fertile, well-drained soil.

HARDINESS Fully hardy/Z4–9

NOTES An award-winning hybrid, this dwarf variety works as a ground cover, in rock gardens or as an edging plant. Another good variety is *H.* 'Chorus Line', with abundant pink flowers through to late summer.

MAINTENANCE Easy. Divide every 3–6 years when clumps become crowded.

ABOVE Passiflora caerulea.

Passiflora caerulea
'Constance Elliot'
BLUE PASSION FLOWER
FAMILY **Passifloraceae**

The flowers of this tendril climber are highly distinctive: ten outer petals surround a crown of central filaments, inside which are the prominent, theatrical stamens. The flowers are white with filaments banded blue, white and purple and are in bloom from mid- to late summer. Most passion flowers are hothouse plants, but *P. c.* is reliably hardy in a sheltered spot in cold areas. It can be evergreen, but if cut down by frosts will usually regenerate from ground level. Can reach a height and spread of 10m (30ft) or more, although this will be less in cooler climates.

CULTIVATION Can be grown in any well-drained soil in sun in a sheltered position. Protect in winter in cold areas. Provide support for tendrils.

HARDINESS Frost hardy/Z8–10

NOTES The creamy white flowers with red stigmas are followed by edible orange fruits.

MAINTENANCE Easy.

Penstemon x gloxinioides
GARDEN PENSTEMON
FAMILY **Scrophulariaceae**

Penstemons are versatile flowers and will grace a rock garden or enhance a perennial border. They have delicate narrow bell-shaped, lipped flowers in a colour range including periwinkle blue, plum, red, pink, white and rarely yellow – these bloom from mid-spring until midsummer. Compact and bushy, they have narrow lance-shaped green leaves, and come in varying heights, up to 1m (3ft).

CULTIVATION Plants like an open, sunny spot with good drainage so if your soil is heavy, add plenty of sand and grit. Roots are sensitive to disturbance and too much moisture, so do not mulch the base of the plant.

HARDINESS Fully to half hardy/Z6–10

NOTES The blossoms are magnets to hummingbirds and butterflies. They will do well in containers with a mixture of multi-purpose potting compost (soil mix) with added grit to aid drainage.

MAINTENANCE Easy. After flowers fade, cut back for repeat blooms.

BELOW Penstemon *x gloxinioides*.

Phlox paniculata
SUMMER PHLOX
FAMILY **Polemoniaceae**

A majestic herbaceous perennial, the elegant flowers start to bloom in mid-summer and are a good choice for providing late summer colour in the garden. The tall flower heads reach up to 1.2m (4ft) high, and produce tubular, scented, white, purple or pink flowers that are ideal for attracting butterflies and moths. Long, mid-green leaves are carried right up the stem; they are lance-shaped with toothed margins.

CULTIVATION Summer phlox will grow in almost any soil but prefers rich, moist but free-draining ground in full sun or semi-shade. Propagate by division in early spring, or basal cuttings can be taken in the spring.

HARDINESS Fully hardy/Z4

NOTES Often used in herbaceous beds, mixed borders or in a specialist butterfly border. The many cultivars include 'Blue Ice' (pale blue), 'Bright Eyes' (pale pink with red eyes), 'Eventide' (pale blue), 'Fujiyama' (pure white), 'Hampton Court' (lilac-blue) and 'Le Mahdi' (violet).

MAINTENANCE Easy.

BELOW Phlox paniculata.

ABOVE Rudbeckia fulgida *var.* sullivantii *'Goldsturm'*.

Rudbeckia fulgida var. *sullivantii* 'Goldsturm'
BLACK-EYED SUSAN
FAMILY **Asteraceae**

An old favourite in cottage gardens, this perennial flowers throughout summer and into the autumn. It grows up to 60cm (2ft) tall with wide, hairy, dark green, lance-shaped leaves. The 7.5cm (3in) yellow flowers with black central cones will brighten the character of any garden.

CULTIVATION This plant can tolerate clay soils and mild droughts, but will thrive in well-drained, moist soil. Does well with high heat and humidity as well as in freezing climates. Plant during the growing season, 45cm (18in) apart, and add mulch to retain moisture.

HARDINESS Fully hardy/Z4–9

NOTES A great cutting flower that reblooms later in the season with bouquets to harvest. Leave seed heads on in the autumn for the birds.

MAINTENANCE Easy. Divide every few years when the plants become crowded. 'Goldsturm' has few pest or disease problems.

Sedum 'Herbstfreude'
SEDUM
FAMILY **Crassulaceae**

This lovely perennial is a succulent with fleshy green leaves about 7.5cm (3in) long. On long, sturdy stems, clusters of pink blossoms show in late summer that age to coppery rust. Bees and butterflies love them. This variety dies completely back in winter. Grows to a height and width of 30–60cm (1–2ft).

CULTIVATION 'Herbstfreude' prefers average to dry, well-drained soil in full sun. Division seems to be the easiest method of propagation. Will tolerate drought.

HARDINESS Fully hardy/Z3–9

NOTES Sedums are native to many parts of the world and come in all sizes, shapes and colours. Some are cold hardy, others are more tender. *S. acre*, the stonecrop, is also hardy and will form a low, dense mat, smothered in yellow flowers for a long period.

MAINTENANCE Easy. Divide clumps every 2–3 years and share the beauty around the garden.

Stachys byzantina
LAMBS' EAR
FAMILY **Lamiaceae**

The texture and colour of this plant's foliage make it ideal for a perennial ground cover. The light purple flowers on tall spikes 30–45cm (12–18in) are not the showiest. It is the leaves' velvety texture and the silvery green colour that get the attention.

CULTIVATION Grow in full sun. This perennial flower thrives in poor soil that is well drained. Its drought-tolerance makes it perfect for rock gardens and a low-maintenance beds.

HARDINESS Fully hardy/Z4–9

NOTES If young children visit your garden this plant will be fun! Just seeing the foliage will spur them to reach out and touch the softness. The leaves press well. Lambs' ear plants are also deer-resistant. Honey bees and other beneficial insects love this plant.

MAINTENANCE Easy. Cut the flower spikes soon after they tend to flop. These plants will spread but removing clumps will keep them under control.

Thunbergia alata
BLACK-EYED SUSAN VINE
FAMILY **Acanthaceae**

This is a cheerful and fresh twining evergreen climber, bearing bright yellow or orange, open flowers, 3–4cm (1¼–1½in) across, with a dark, tubular centre. If grown as a perennial (kept warm over winter), it reaches 2.5m (8ft) high, as an annual 1.5–2m (5–7ft).

CULTIVATION Set plants out in a sunny location after the last frost and when the weather is warm. This vine needs regular water and rich, well-drained soil.

HARDINESS Half hardy/Z10–11

NOTES Does well in containers and in the ground. The latter will encourage it to really take off. Train on to strings or install low trellis if in a container.

MAINTENANCE Easy.

Viola x *wittrockiana* cultivars
PANSY
FAMILY **Violaceae**

A 'flower for all seasons', pansies are perennials usually grown as annuals, and some varieties will flower right through mild winters. Pansy blooms are single with five petals that are rounded in shape. The coarsely notched leaves are medium green, oval or heart-shaped. Grows to a height of 15–25cm (6–10in).

CULTIVATION Need rich, fertile soil, so add manure, leafmould or compost and turn it several times. They like sun in the morning and dappled shade in hot afternoons. Regular water is adequate.

HARDINESS Fully hardy/Z4–8

NOTES Another variety to try is *V. odorata*, the old-fashioned, very fragrant violet. It only reaches 20cm (8in) high, so you need to get close to get the full scent. Another is *V. alba*, the Parma Violet variety, less hardy than the others, but is intensely scented and does well in containers. Pansy blossoms are easy to press and beautiful to use on cards and bookmarks for craft projects.

MAINTENANCE Very easy. Just remember to take time to deadhead.

BELOW *Viola* x *wittrockiana*.

ABOVE Zinnia elegans.

Zinnia elegans
ZINNIA
FAMILY **Asteraceae**

If sown successively, zinnias will give you flowers over a long period in summer. The leaves are lance-shaped and sandpaper-like in texture. Hybrids come in dwarf, intermediate and tall varieties. Flowers range from tiny button-like heads to large heads with double petals, in almost every colour except blue. Depending on the variety, height varies from 60–65cm (2–2½ft).

CULTIVATION Choose a site in full sun, although zinnias like a little afternoon shade in especially hot regions. Provide rich, well-drained soil. Keep soil somewhat moist by mulching. They can survive in soil that's on the dry side but will wilt in very dry conditions.

HARDINESS Half hardy/Z3–10

MAINTENANCE Easy. To produce bushier plants, pinch the tops out of young plants when they are 10–15cm (4–6in) high. Remove faded blossoms during the season to keep them producing. 'Cut and Come' will give many weeks of blooms if you keep harvesting it.

FLOWERS AND PLANTS THAT THRIVE IN THE SHADE

Defining the word 'shade' can be a lively and complex vocabulary game. The dimly lit area beneath evergreens will be different from the space under or near deciduous shrubs and trees. The terms used here are 'light shade' where there is a predominance of lightly dappled shade cast by trees and shrubs, 'partial shade' where there is four to six hours of more heavily filtered sunlight from surrounding trees or shrubs and 'full shade' where there is less than four hours of daily sunlight and dense shade from trees and shrubs.

ABOVE Asarum caudatum, *a dark green ground cover of heart-shaped leaves, creates a spicy, gingery perfume.*

Alchemilla mollis
LADY'S MANTLE
FAMILY Rosaceae

This charming perennial does well in sun or partial shade. The sweetly scented yellowish-green flowers seem to float above the soft-looking scallop-edged foliage, which has a bluish cast. Reaches 50cm (20in).

CULTIVATION Lady's mantle prefers moist, humus-rich soil, but will tolerate drought. It likes an application of mulch, which keeps it cool and moist. Root dividing or digging up the volunteer plants will let you share them generously. If they become messy or too numerous, simply divide them or thin them out.

HARDINESS Fully hardy/Z4–8

NOTES The velvety leaves hold beads of water on their surfaces that look like tiny round diamonds. The flower clusters nicely accent bouquets.

MAINTENANCE Easy. It can naturalize easily when it drops its many seeds, so keep it deadheaded if you do not want multiple plants in odd places.

Asarum
WILD GINGER
FAMILY Aristolochiaceae

This attractive, fast-growing ground cover forms lush carpets of green heart-shaped, leathery leaves. Spring bloom brings unique but shy bell-shaped brownish-red flowers that are tucked under the leaves. In a naturalistic setting such as a woodland shade garden, this plant complements the evergreens and wildflowers.

CULTIVATION Because this plant is native to woodland settings, it really wants full shade. Wild ginger can grow in heavy soils with lots of water but prefers a looser humus-rich soil that is slightly acidic.

HARDINESS Fully hardy/Z6–8

NOTES Roots and leaves have scent similar to culinary ginger but should not be used as seasoning. Look for varieties that provide silvery markings, such as *A. shuttleworthii,* which lends interest to the front edges of a garden, and *A. caudatum,* which is evergreen and more drought-tolerant.

MAINTENANCE Easy. However, you may have to protect the plant from slugs and drying winds. Feel free to divide this plant in the spring or autumn – you will have plenty of divisions to share!

LEFT Alchemilla mollis.

ABOVE Aspidistra elatior.

Aspidistra elatior
CAST-IRON PLANT
FAMILY Liliaceae

Though a popular Victorian houseplant, this sturdy long-lived plant can be a staple for the shade garden. With its wide, lance-shaped, leathery, evergreen leaves it makes a striking accent to the outdoor garden. It will reach 30–60cm (1–2ft) high and wide.

CULTIVATION The cast-iron plant likes a moist but well-drained, fertile, sandy soil. It can survive in hard, poor soils, but it won't tolerate soggy conditions and if in the direct sun the foliage will burn and turn brown. It needs a sheltered position, and should be protected in cold winters with fleece or similar.

HARDINESS Frost tender/Z7–10

NOTES The leaves of the cast-iron plant are especially long-lasting in flower arrangements.

MAINTENANCE Easy. Aspidistra thrives on neglect and will do fine unless the soil is practically devoid of nutrients, so fertilize during period of active growth for the best appearance. Red spider mites might need to be controlled.

Astilbe
ASTILBE, FALSE SPIREA
FAMILY Saxifragaceae

This light, airy plant that carries feather-like flowers on slender and wiry stems is a treasure in the shade. The dark green, delicately cut leaflets give a foundation to the rise of small white, pink or red plume-like flowers. If not deadheaded, the flowerheads turn an attractive shade of brown and look good throughout the winter. They can grow from 15–90cm (6in–3ft) or taller.

CULTIVATION Astilbe likes moist, humus-rich soil. If the site is consistently moist, or even boggy, it will thrive in full sun; in drier soil it does best in partial shade. It will tolerate full shade but bloom may not be as robust.

HARDINESS Fully hardy/Z5–8

NOTES Look for the drought-tolerant variety, *A. chinensis*, which grows to 60cm (2ft) high and wide, and has dense, pinkish-white flowers in late summer. *A.* 'Deutchland', at 50cm (20in) high, produces its white flowers in late spring.

MAINTENANCE Easy. Will benefit from being fed during the summer. Deadhead faded flowering stems and every 4 or 5 years divide the clumps.

BELOW Astilbe.

ABOVE Begonia *x* tuberhybrida *'Non-Stop'*.

Begonia x *tuberhybrida*
BEGONIA
FAMILY Begoniaceae

This tender, winter-dormant perennial tolerates little light and is a bonus to a shade garden. Tuberous begonias offer a rainbow of colours on single- or double-frilled or plain petals and bloom all summer. Some grow upright with large, arrow-shaped leaves on brittle stems to 75cm (30in). Pendula begonias are ideal for hanging baskets on a shady tree limb.

CULTIVATION Tuberous begonias grow best in light shade or the foliage will scorch. They need rich, well-drained soil high in organic matter. Allow soil to dry between waterings.

HARDINESS Frost tender/Z10

NOTES Begonias are divided into a different types and groups, with flowers in almost every colour except blue, and including some that bloom through the winter. *B.* 'Can-Can' is an upright Tuberhybrida type, whose yellow flowers have a striking, frilly, pinkish-red edge.

MAINTENANCE Moderate. To encourage continued bloom and shape, keep deadheading and pinching back leggy stems. To save tubers for next year, dig them up and store in a cool, dry area.

ABOVE Campanula persicifolia.

Campanula persicifolia
PEACH-LEAF RED BELLFLOWER
FAMILY **Campanulaceae**

Bellflowers are a group of plants that light up a garden with their bright blue flowers that grow on long, slender, flexible stems. Heights (including other species) vary from 60–1.8m (2–6ft). The flowers appear in early summer and, as the name implies, the leaves of *C. persicifolia* look very like the leaves of a peach tree.

CULTIVATION Grow in light shade or full sun. These plants love cool summers and regular water. Native to open woods, they like well-drained soil that is high in organic matter.

HARDINESS Fully hardy/Z4–8

NOTES The variety *C. carpatica*, known as Carpathian harebell, is a delight since it stays low 15–30cm (6–12in) and is long blooming. Add to a rock garden or as a bed border.

MAINTENANCE Easy. Watch for slugs.

Cyclamen
SOWBREAD
FAMILY **Primulaceae**

This delightful genus is native to the Mediterranean. The flowers are unique and distinctive, with their swept-back petals. The hardy species of cyclamen are invaluable in the garden, as they belong to a select group of plants that thrive in dry shade and are therefore excellent for planting beneath trees, where in time they will build up large colonies. The leaves are usually beautifully marked.

CULTIVATION Prefers moderately fertile, moist but well-drained soil in partial shade, but will tolerate drier soils.

HARDINESS Hardy/Z5–10

NOTES *C. coum* flowers from late winter to mid-spring, in a variety of colours from purple-violet to pink and white. *C. persicum* has scented flowers that appear in winter and spring.

MAINTENANCE Easy. An annual mulch of leaf mould is beneficial.

BELOW Cyclamen coum.

Dicentra spectabilis
BLEEDING HEART
FAMILY **Pavaveraceae**

This is perennial favourite of partially shaded gardens. The common bleeding heart has lobed green foliage that gives a delicate feel to this plant, which grows up to 75cm (30in). The key features are the abundant red heart-shaped flowers that hang from arching stems.

CULTIVATION They thrive in partial shade with rich, moist and slightly acidic soil. It should not be too wet. They bloom later in the spring and into early summer. Foliage dies down even in mild climates, but in hotter climates the plant usually lasts for just one season.

HARDINESS Fully hardy/Z4–8

NOTES These flowers are a visual treat and are wonderful to press.

ABOVE Dicentra spectabilis.

MAINTENANCE Easy. When blooming is finally over, the foliage will turn yellow and the plant can then be cut to the ground. Plant flowering annuals to fill the areas.

Epimedium grandiflorum
BISHOP'S HAT, FAIRY WINGS
FAMILY **Berberidaceae**

An excellent perennial ground cover in shady areas. The heart-shaped foliage is attractive all year round and grows on stems 7.5–10cm (3–4in) high. The leaves are light green, but in the spring will have a pink to bronze tint. The foliage will remain all winter if the plant is in a protected location. In late spring, star-shaped, four-petalled flowers dangle in clusters and, depending on the cultivar, they may be white, cream, rose, lavender or yellow in colour.

CULTIVATION Does its best when grown in light to partial shade. Prefers a rich, moist, well-drained soil, with the addition of compost and leafmould. Epimediums are propagated by division in the spring or autumn.

HARDINESS Fully hardy/Z5–9

NOTES A great ground cover under trees because it will happily cohabit.

MAINTENANCE Easy.

Galium odoratum
SWEET WOODRUFF
FAMILY **Rubiaceae**

This perennial ground cover is best suited for informal plantings with its white, star-shaped fragrant flowers that bloom in mid-spring atop stems that are covered with shiny, whorled leaves. Reaches a height of 15cm (6in) and spreads to 30cm (12in) or more.

CULTIVATION Grows well in full shade and moist, well-drained soil. Too much sun will stunt the plant and it may die back.

HARDINESS Fully hardy/Z5–8

NOTES The whole plant is fragrant and brushing against it will release its fresh odour. The plant was often used to flavour May wine and in medieval times the most fragrant variety, *G. verum*, was used to stuff mattresses, which is why another common name is 'bedstraw'.

MAINTENANCE Easy. Prune plant back in spring to prevent it from getting too leggy. In cold areas, winter protection is recommended.

BELOW Epimedium grandiflorum.

BELOW Galium odoratum.

Gaultheria procumbens
WINTERGREEN
FAMILY Ericaceae

This versatile evergreen ground cover has upright stems about 5–15cm (2–6in) high with oval glossy dark green leaves. When bruised, the leaves emit a strong wintergreen fragrance. Scarlet berries follow urn-shaped summer flowers of pinkish white.

CULTIVATION With light to full shade, this plant will thrive in rich, moist, acidic soil. While wintergreen can tolerate some drought, it will keep looking its best with regular watering.

HARDINESS Fully hardy/Z3–8

NOTES Wintergreen was once widely used as a medicinal herb, both externally and as a tea, and the oil was used to flavour root beer and toothpaste. It is still used in making perfumes. The plant is an effective ground cover, spreading by rhizomes to form mats 1m (3ft) across.

MAINTENANCE Easy. A regular mulch of conifer needles will help to increase the soil's acidity.

BELOW Geranium macrorrhizum.

ABOVE Gaultheria procumbens.

Geranium macrorrhizum
CRANESBILL
FAMILY Geraniaceae

This cottage garden favourite forms an attractive ground cover through summer and autumn. It is an excellent perennial, clump forming and spreading by rhizomes. It typically grows 30–38cm (12–15in) tall and can spread to 60cm (24in). Five-petalled, deep magenta flowers with dark red sepals, 2.5cm (1in) across, appear in clusters above the foliage from mid- to late spring and may rebloom later. The palmate, deeply lobed (5–7 lobes), medium green leaves (basal leaves 10–20cm/4–8in wide) are hairy, sticky and aromatic.

CULTIVATION Easy to grow in average, dry to medium, well-drained soil in part shade. Tolerates drought due to thick rhizomes as well as hot and humid summers. The removal of flowering stems is all that is usually necessary for maintaining an attractive plant appearance. If foliage decline occurs as the summer progresses, individual leaves may be removed as they yellow. If flowering stems are not removed, some self-seeding may occur in ideal growing conditions.

HARDINESS Fully hardy/Z4–8

NOTES This plant is sometimes called bigroot or bigfoot geranium due to its thick, fleshy rhizomes. The leaves acquire attractive red and bronze tints in the autumn. Flowers give way to cranesbill-like seed heads. A multi-season plant.

MAINTENANCE Easy. It makes such a dense ground cover that it chokes out most weeds. Good news – plants of this species do not need to be cut back, sheared or otherwise trimmed after flowering.

Helleborus orientalis
LENTEN ROSE
FAMILY Ranunculaceae

This evergreen perennial enlivens a shade garden with handsome and glossy dark green leaves that are finely serrated. This plant can stand alone as a showpiece or be joined by others in scattered groupings in a woodland scene. The Lenten rose gets its name from it approximate bloom time – early spring – with 5–10cm (2–4in) single white or pink rose-type flowers that seem to rise out of the soil without any connection to the foliage. They last for many weeks and as they age some flowers turn pinkish green or purple. Since the flowers hang downwards and are often hidden under the leaves, some people like to grow them in raised beds or containers, or to remove some of the leaves – though this does weaken the plants.

ABOVE Hosta fortunei aureomarginata.

Hosta
PLANTAIN LILY
FAMILY **Liliaceae**

Hostas are grown for their lush foliage in heart, lance, oval and even round shapes in colours from dark green to chartreuse, grey or blue, with many variegated versions. The delicate spikes of flowers rise form the centre of the clump in summer, in pastel shades of pink, purple, cream and white.

CULTIVATION Grow in rich, consistently moist but well-drained soil in a shady, sheltered site.

HARDINESS Fully hardy/Z4–9

NOTES Hostas are good container plants, too. Those with textured or waxy leaves tend to attract fewer pests. Leaves make long-lasting and wonderful additions to cut flower arrangements. The patriot hosta (*H. fortunei*) is an especially good beginner plant.

MAINTENANCE Easy. However, protect them from slugs and snails. Those with textured or waxy leaves attract fewer pests. Plants go completely dormant in the winter, collapsing to a pile of yellow leaves. Remove these and wait for their re-emergence in late spring.

BELOW Heuchera sanguinea *'Monet'*.

CULTIVATION Hellebores will do well in light shade and prefer rich, moist and well-drained soil. Lots of organic material will keep this nourished since feeding it nitrogen may damage the roots. It grows slowly from spreading rhizomes and is not invasive.

HARDINESS Fully to half hardy/Z5–9

NOTES A warning: the variety *H. niger*, the Christmas rose, while just as lovely as the Lenten rose, is highly toxic to humans and animals.

MAINTENANCE Moderate. Feed once or twice a year. Try not to move since it takes them several years to re-establish after transplanting. In early spring clip the over-wintered foliage as close to the ground as possible.

Heuchera sanguinea
CORAL BELLS
FAMILY **Saxifragaceae**

A versatile plant for a rockery, shady border or container. It forms a tidy clump of scalloped, round leaves, 7.5–15cm (3–6in) high. The delicate clusters of large, red, tubular flowers are borne on tall, wiry stems and brighten a low-light area. *H. s.* is ideal for a border front in dappled shade.

CULTIVATION Plant in sun or partial shade in rich, fertile soil and set the crowns above soil level. The leaves are likely to scorch in full sun. They can tolerate some drought once established but excellent drainage is critical in the winter.

HARDINESS Fully to frost hardy/Z3–9

NOTES *H.* 'Santa Anna Cardinal' has vibrant rose-red flowers over a long period in summer. This variety is a delight to see and to add to bouquets. It is attractive to bees, hummingbirds and butterflies.

MAINTENANCE Moderate. Annual mulching is recommended, since the rootstock tends to push upwards. It is best to lift and replant every few years, or replace with new plants. In a mild climate, watch for mealy bugs at the base of the plants.

ABOVE *A formal edging border with* Impatiens walleriana.

Impatiens walleriana
BUSY LIZZIE
FAMILY **Balsaminaceae**
Mostly tender annuals or perennials, busy Lizzies are a universally popular bedding plant, grown for their brightly coloured flowers, produced over a long period. They come in all colours apart from yellow and blue (bright red, orange, pink, purple, violet or white) and have narrow glossy green leaves on succulent pale-green stems.
CULTIVATION Grow them in partial shade in fertile but well-drained, humus-rich soils in cool sites. They can be pinched back to encourage bushiness or planted slightly closer. They require constant moisture levels but not standing water.
HARDINESS Half hardy/Z10–11
NOTES Look for the many cultivars, including the Super Elfin and Tempo Series, including doubles, variegated leaves, and uprights.
MAINTENANCE Easy.

Lamium maculatum
SPOTTED DEAD NETTLE
FAMILY **Lamiaceae**
Spotted dead nettle is a popular ground cover because of its silvery foliage that brightens up dark, shady areas. With a height of up to 15cm (6in), it is a low spreader, 20cm (8in) wide, with variegated 2.5cm (1in) crinkle leaves with rounded teeth. Lavender flowers with upper and lower lips bloom from spring to late summer. These plants can tolerate shady areas that have dry soil.
CULTIVATION Plant spotted dead nettles in an evenly moist, well-drained, moderately rich soil in partial shade. They prefer cool temperatures.
HARDINESS Fully hardy/Z4–8
NOTES The metallic hue on the leaves makes this useful for designs with creative colour schemes. The 'White Nancy' variety stays relatively short – only 15cm (6in) – but spreads to 1m (3ft) or more. 'Anne Greenway' offers an exquisite blend of chartreuse, silver, medium-green and mint green foliage, making this ground cover breathtaking even when not in bloom.
MAINTENANCE Moderate. It is best to cut this plant back after the first bloom to promote compact growth.

Pachysandra procumbens
PACHYSANDRA, ALLEGHENY SPURGE
FAMILY **Buxaceae**
This ground cover gives clean and compact growth with grey-green oval leaves. It reaches 1.8–3.6m (6–12ft) high. The two-toned foliage is richly patterned and persists through most winters. A second-storey layering of fresh green leaves follows the fragrant white flowers that appear briefly in the spring. They do not compete with tree roots so are perfect for hugging around a shady tree trunk. Can be evergreen or deciduous.
CULTIVATION Ideal for shady areas in moist, acidic soil. Plant 2.5cm (1in) apart as they spread by underground runners.
HARDINESS Fully hardy/Z4–8
NOTES Handles full shade or part sun but too much sun will hamper growth and turn leaves yellow. Each year give bed well amended organic mulching.
MAINTENANCE Easy.

BELOW Lamium maculatum.

Polygonatum biflorum
SOLOMON'S SEAL
FAMILY Liliaceae

This woodland perennial fills the back areas of gardens with grace and elegance. The stems tend to arch and lean over to one side. Leaves are 15cm (6in) long and 10cm (4in) wide and are spaced close together along the stem. From late spring to midsummer, small, white, bell-shaped flowers hang in pairs from the leaf axils. Bluish-black berries appear once the flowers are finished. Grows to a height of 1.5m (5ft) or more.

CULTIVATION Grow in full or partial shade, in fertile, loamy soil. Fairly rugged, the plant will tolerate less than ideal conditions but does best with regular water. Foliage persists all summer.

HARDINESS Fully hardy/Z3–8

NOTES Occurs in both high-quality and degraded woodlands, which makes it a versatile garden plant. The nectar and pollen of the flowers attract various bees, including bumblebees, and the Ruby-throated hummingbird, which also sucks the nectar from the flowers.

MAINTENANCE Easy. The plant dies down after the first frost and rises again in spring warmth. It grows from thick, fleshy rhizomes that can be divided and transplanted. The leaves are often damaged by slugs and sawfly larvae, but the plants usually recover, once established.

Polystichum acrostichoides
CHRISTMAS FERN
FAMILY Dryopteriaceae

Dark evergreen leaves that grow 30–45cm (1–1½ft) tall in symmetrical clumps about 90cm (3ft) wide. Looks best when mixed with other woodland type plants. Fronds stay upright and offer lovely contrast to snow in colder climates. In spring, lovely light green fiddleheads emerge.

CULTIVATION Grow in rich well-drained soils in mixed woodland plantings or against a wall in shady areas.

ABOVE Polygonatum biflorum.

HARDINESS Fully hardy/Z3

NOTES There are many other species with interesting frond shapes, colours and textures. Florists use the fronds for fresh and dried arrangements.

MAINTENANCE Easy. Cut old fronds before fiddleheads emerge to keep tidy.

Primula
PRIMROSE
FAMILY Primulaceae

Every shade garden needs to host a collection of primroses. They are valued for their colourful spring blooms as well as the textured green round or oblong leaves that form a tight, rosette base.

CULTIVATION Does well in partial shade and grown in organically enriched soil that is slightly acidic and well drained. They do best in cool and humid climates.

HARDINESS Fully hardy to frost tender/Z5–6

NOTES Varieties include P. helodoxa, with its small umbels of rose or lilac flowers, P. japonica with its tubular, deep red flowers, and P. vulgaris with its flat, soft yellow flowers. Don't forget P. veris, better known as cowslip, with nodding clusters of fragrant yellow flowers.

MAINTENANCE Easy, especially in areas with chilly winters and cool summers. Deadhead to ensure longer blooming. In the autumn, dig and divide overcrowded clumps.

Solenostemon
COLEUS
FAMILY Lamiaceae

Grown for its vividly coloured leaves in many patterns, this tropical plant is a tender perennial that will be killed by the first frost. Sizes range from 60cm (2ft) tall to dwarf versions. The large leaves do particularly well in the shade. While the blue flower spikes are attractive, they are often pruned since they detract from the plant's shape.

CULTIVATION Plant outdoors when temperatures are warm in neutral pH, moist and well-drained soil. Propagate from stem cuttings or seeds.

HARDINESS Frost tender/Z10

NOTES Great for borders, indoor and outdoor containers. The hybrid Kong Series comes in vibrant reds, roses, mosaics and scarlet.

MAINTENANCE Easy. Late summer blooms should be pinched off to encourage leaf growth. Highly resistant to disease or insect problems. Feed regularly with nitrogen-rich fertilizer.

BELOW Primula japonica.

TREES AND SHRUBS THAT PREFER FULL SUN

If your garden is a sunshine oasis, a mixture of sun and shade, or has a sun-drenched wall or corner, then you will need trees and shrubs that will thrive there. Here is a selection of those that do well in the sun, others that can cope with alternating sun and shade and all with preferences for soil and moisture conditions that can be chosen to suit your climate. From the drought-tolerant abelia and the fragrant Chinese witch hazel, to the cool-climate-loving blue spruce and the Californian lilac with its intense violet flowers, here is a sampling to inspire you.

ABOVE Amelanchier arborea *(common serviceberry) is well suited to small gardens and has a mass of white spring blossoms.*

Abelia x grandiflora 'Little Richard'
ABELIA
FAMILY Caprifoliaceae

This mounding, compact shrub may be semi-evergreen depending on climate and has clusters of small white bell-shaped flowers from summer right through the autumn. Grows 3m (10ft) high and wide.

CULTIVATION A non-complaining shrub, abelia thrives in soils from clay to loam. It is drought- and salt-tolerant. Does well in full sun but also performs well in light shade.

HARDINESS Half hardy/Z6–9

NOTES Wildlife such as hummingbirds

BELOW Abelia *x* grandiflora *'Little Richard'.*

and butterflies love this shrub. Foliage turns a deep copper colour, adding to its already impressive winter display.

MAINTENANCE Easy. Do not shear but select a few branches and prune at ground level. This selective pruning will open the centre and give better shape.

Amelanchier arborea
SERVICEBERRY, JUNEBERRY, SHAD BUSH
FAMILY Rosaceae

This small tree offers four seasons of interest with white and fragrant spring flowers with showy white petals that occur in elongated, drooping bunches. Red to purple round berries hang in small clusters as they ripen in early to

midsummer. The fruits are edible, so are a great attraction for birds. It has wonderful autumn colours ranging from bright yellow, peach and apricot to orange and deep red. Plant with an evergreen backdrop and create a lovely landscape scene. Can reach a height of 10m (30ft) with a narrow spread.

CULTIVATION Grow in an average, medium, well-drained soil in full sun to part shade. It is tolerant of a wide range of soils and needs regular watering.

HARDINESS Fully hardy/Z5–9

NOTES Edible berries can make great pies if you can harvest them before the birds steal them.

MAINTENANCE Easy.

Ceanothus thyrsiflorus
CALIFORNIAN LILAC
FAMILY Rhamnaceae

Small, glossy, dark green holly-like leaves are abundant on this low-growing evergreen shrub. Dark violet blue 2.5cm (1in) clusters of flowers cover it in early spring. Reaches a height of 60–90cm (2–3ft) and a width of 2.5–3m (8–10ft). Other good varieties are *C. gloriosus exultatus* 'Emily Brown' (ground cover), *C.* 'Gloire de Versailles' and *C.* 'Concha'.

CULTIVATION Give them light, well-drained soil and occasional summer watering. They do tolerate heavy soil.

HARDINESS Frost hardy/Z7–9

NOTES Provides habitat and cover for songbirds as well as seeds eaten by

bushtits, mockingbirds, quail and finches. Attracts bees and bumblebees.
MAINTENANCE Easy. Control growth by tip pruning during growing season.

Cornus kousa
KOUSA DOGWOOD
FAMILY **Cornaceae**

This small deciduous ornamental tree has dense growth with delicate limbs that spread horizontally. It bears white, star-shaped flower-like bracts in late spring to early summer. Showy red fruits that look like a big, round raspberry persist throughout the summer. The autumn foliage colour is red to maroon. Even the bark offers special interest in that initially it is smooth and light brown but as it ages it exfoliates into small patches forming a tan and brown camouflage pattern. Can reach 7m (22ft) in height.
CULTIVATION This dogwood likes to grow in in full or partial sun. It is a slow grower, with very low water requirements, and has tolerance for salty soils.
HARDINESS Fully hardy/Z5–8
NOTES *C. k.* var. *chinensis* has larger flower heads and more narrowly pointed bracts. The berries are edible and wild birds love them.

BELOW *Cornus kousa*.

ABOVE Euonymus alatus *'Fireball'*.

MAINTENANCE Easy. This is a good choice because it is resistant to typical dogwood anthracnose disease and dogwood borer moth.

Euonymus alatus
BURNING BUSH
FAMILY **Celastraceae**

This deciduous twiggy shrub that grows to a height of only 3m (10ft) and a width of 90cm–1.5m (3–5ft) accents a landscape for several seasons. The summer foliage is dark green and the shrub will do best in full sun. It's drought-tolerant after the first year of getting established but not if in a container. Waiting for its brilliant autumn show of fiery red foliage, however, is one of the reasons to have this in your garden.
CULTIVATION Plant in full sun to achieve vibrant autumn colour. It is tolerant of a variety of soils.
HARDINESS Fully hardy/Z4–9
MAINTENANCE Easy. If you choose to prune to keep its shape, do so in the autumn or early winter after the leaves fall. When shaping, prune out the entire branch, removing it from the base of the plant.

Hamamelis mollis
CHINESE WITCH HAZEL
FAMILY **Hamamelidaceae**

This slow-growing small deciduous tree or shrub can reach up to 4m (12ft) high. It presents a vase-shaped silhouette with bare outstretched limbs waiting for the early and lovely yellow spring flowers to adorn them. They are fragrant and have been described as looking like shredded coconut or spiders.
CULTIVATION Thrives in well-drained, fertile, humus-rich soil, in full sun. It also grows well under the bright shade of tall trees or with a half day of sun and a half day of shade. Provide regular water during summer dry spells, watering deeply to encourage a deep and extensive root system.
HARDINESS Fully hardy/Z5–9
NOTES This wonderful tree/shrub has many interesting features but its spring and autumn displays are perhaps their periods of crowning glory. You can bring in a branch in winter and force the fragrant flowers to bloom indoors.
MAINTENANCE Easy. Prune only to guide its shape and growth or to remove suckers.

BELOW Hamamelis mollis *'Pallida'*.

ABOVE Lagerstroemia indica.

Lagerstroemia indica
CRAPE MYRTLE
FAMILY Lythraceae

This four-season deciduous tree is a treasure. It comes in sizes to fit large or small spaces and has showy flowers and bark as well as great autumn colour and winter fruit. Flowers are borne in summer in big clusters and come in white and many shades of pink, purple, lavender and red. The fruits that follow are brown or black. When mature they dry and split, releasing disc-shaped seeds.

CULTIVATION Provide moist soil and it will grow rapidly, but once established it will tolerate dry conditions. Careful pruning is recommended to remove crossing or overly dense branches.
HARDINESS Frost hardy/Z7–10
NOTES Look for the newer varieties which can survive in colder temperatures.
MAINTENANCE Easy. Prune lightly in the dormant season.

Oxydendrum arboreum
SOURWOOD, SORREL TREE
FAMILY Ericaceae

An exquisite four-season slow-growing deciduous tree. It has drooping, long-lasting sprays of fragrant flowers in early to midsummer and lights up the garden with its soft red, luminescent maroon and yellow foliage in autumn. If this is not enough, add the pyramidal pendulous branches, chunky bark, reddish new wood and shimmery spring leaves, and you have an outstanding specimen tree. Grows to about 15m (50ft) high and 7.5m (25ft) wide.

CULTIVATION Propagate by softwood cuttings in summer or by seed in autumn. Thrives in acidic, richly organic soil. Roots are shallow, so avoid planting under the tree or use ground covers that are shallow rooted. Cooler summers are best for this tree.
HARDINESS Fully hardy/Z5–9
MAINTENANCE Easy.

Picea pungens 'Baby Blue Eyes'
BLUE SPRUCE, COLORADO SPRUCE
FAMILY Pinaceae

A slow-growing pyramidal semi-dwarf tree with sky-blue stiff needles in neat rows. The rough grey bark adds texture to the landscape. Can reach 15m (50ft) high and 5m (15ft) wide.

CULTIVATION Does best in full sun to part shade. Give it moderate water and rich, well-drained soil. The shallow root system likes cool climates.
HARDINESS Fully hardy/Z3–8
NOTES Ideal as an accent tree for small areas. Birds are attracted to spruces for shelter and food.
MAINTENANCE Easy. Resistant to spider mite. Needs no pruning since it grows only 5–7.5cm (2–3in) per year.

Stewartia pseudocamellia
JAPANESE STEWARTIA
FAMILY Theaceae

This excellent four-season deciduous garden tree grows slowly to 20m (70ft) tall and 6–9m (25–30ft) wide. Pyramid shaped, it is often multi-trunked. Older bark exfoliates creating a camouflage pattern of orange, green and grey. The deep green foliage is elliptical with finely serrated margins.

CULTIVATION Grows best in humus-rich, acidic soils with good drainage and even moisture. Mulch in light soils and during dry seasons.
HARDINESS Fully hardy/Z7–9
NOTES A good showpiece tree in woodland gardens. Throughout the summer it bears white camellia-like flowers with orange anthers. Autumn foliage turns orange, red and then purple. A brown pointed triangular fruit appears and persists, giving winter interest.
MAINTENANCE Easy. Needs little to no care beyond the removal at intervals of weak and exhausted wood.

BELOW Stewartia pseudocamellia.

TREES AND SHRUBS THAT THRIVE IN THE SHADE

As gardens come in all shapes and sizes, their rates of exposure to the sun also differ widely. The location, the landscape design, its proximity to other buildings, and the growth of trees over time can create a garden that is defined by shade. While tending a garden with little direct sun may be challenging, with research, nursery shopping and observation of local gardens, you can find interesting trees and shrubs that will thrive in such conditions. Moreover, tending a shade garden is often less work and always offers a cool and relaxing spot to rest in.

ABOVE Calycanthus *is a versatile four-season shrub – enjoy the spicy, cinnamon aroma of the burgundy flowers and bark.*

Acer circinatum
VINE MAPLE
FAMILY Aceraceae

This deciduous tree can grow in the understorey of moist forests where its shape is often sprawling and crooked. In open areas it is more of a symmetrical small tree that has an upright habit. Lovely greenish-red circular leaves turn orange and scarlet in the autumn. Perfect for a woodland landscape surrounded by ferns. Grows up to 5m (15ft) or more.

CULTIVATION Needs an evenly moist, well-drained soil, and moderate water.

HARDINESS Fully hardy/Z6–9

NOTES A four-season jewel for a shady garden – the twisty, leafless branches offer delicate patterns against a winter sky.

MAINTENANCE Easy. Prune in late autumn to midwinter.

Acer palmatum
JAPANESE MAPLE
FAMILY Aceraceae

This small, slow-growing deciduous tree has year-long interest. Early spring growth glows red and the delicately cut green leaves turn brilliant colours in the autumn. Height and spread of 6m (20ft).

CULTIVATION Growth is best in moist, well-drained soils that are high in organic matter. Give protection from hot, drying winds. They are happy with conditions that have filtered sunlight. Because they are shallow rooted, do not cultivate the surrounding soil and avoid planting them near established shallow rooted trees (such as beech or large maples). Mulch to prevent weeds.

HARDINESS Fully hardy/Z5–8

NOTES With so many varieties, this is an enjoyable tree to research.

MAINTENANCE Moderate. Prune lightly if it becomes too big.

Calycanthus occidentalis
SPICE BUSH, CALIFORNIA ALLSPICE
FAMILY Calycanthaceae

This clump-forming deciduous shrub is perfect as a background plant or for giving privacy to a space. It can reach 3m (10ft) high and wide. Leaves start out a lime-green colour and darken through summer and then turn yellow in the autumn. Late spring or early summer brings brownish red flowers that resemble small water lilies. Both foliage and blossoms have fragrance.

CULTIVATION This shrub can be trained to be a multi-stemmed tree. Likes shade or sun and regular water. Can tolerate sand, clay, poor drainage and seasonal flooding.

HARDINESS Fully hardy/Z6–9

NOTES Easily grown from seeds, but the seeds are toxic, so be cautious.

MAINTENANCE Easy. Remove twiggy stems annually to tidy. Avoid hard pruning.

BELOW Acer palmatum '*Nicholsonii*'.

Camellia sasanqua
WINTER-BLOOMING CAMELLIA
FAMILY Theaceae

These broad-leaved evergreen shrubs will make you smile on a dark winter's day. Flowers are produced in late autumn and winter along stems with shiny, dark green leaves. Blossoms come in single, double and semi-double forms. These are fragrant and come in pastel pinks, roses and whites, with a few of them deep rose, deep pink and bright red. Growth ranges from 45cm–3.6m (1½–12ft) high and 1.8–3.6m (6–12ft) wide.

CULTIVATION Likes well-drained, acidic soil rich in organic material – older plants are fairly drought-tolerant but younger ones like regular watering with rainwater.

HARDINESS Frost hardy/Z7–9

NOTES Tolerates more sun than other varieties. They can be trained onto a trellis and do well in pots.

MAINTENANCE Easy. Prune after flowering. In the spring, keep roots cool by placing 5cm (2in) of mulch that does not touch the trunk base.

Cornus stolonifera 'Flaviramea'
RED TWIG DOGWOOD
FAMILY Cornaceae

This woody, deciduous, multi-limbed shrub is grown for its stunning red

BELOW Camellia sasanqua.

ABOVE Cornus stolonifera.

autumn foliage and winter twig display. Grows 2.1–2.75m (7–9ft) high and spreads 3.6m (12ft), but pruning can manage shape. Summertime creamy white flowers appear in 5cm (2in) clusters that later bear white or bluish berries. Truly a plant for all seasons.

CULTIVATION Thrives in cold and warm temperatures. Tolerates poor soil but will do better with moderate water. Cut down severely in winter while dormant.

HARDINESS Fully hardy/Z2–8

NOTES Good for preventing soil erosion and space filling. Lovely against a pale-coloured wall in the winter as the red bark lights up the area.

MAINTENANCE Easy. Spreads by underground runner, so use a spade to cut off roots.

Hydrangea quercifolia
OAK-LEAF HYDRANGEA
FAMILY Hydrangeaceae

A four-season shrub that reaches 2m (6ft) tall and wide. Has attractive, deeply lobed leaves that resemble those of oaks, and gives fabulous autumn colour. It bears large elongated clusters of white flowers in late spring and early summer. They turn a lovely pinkish-maroon by the autumn.

CULTIVATION The perfect exposure will get morning sun and afternoon shade.

Needs excellent drainage in slightly acidic soil, but withstands hotter temperatures than other varieties.

HARDINESS Frost hardy/Z5–9

NOTES 'Sikes Dwarf' and 'Pee Wee' work well in smaller gardens.

MAINTENANCE Easy. During dry spells it will appreciate regular deep waterings about twice a week.

Kalmia latifolia
MOUNTAIN LAUREL, CALICO BUSH
FAMILY Ericaceae

This slow-growing handsome evergreen shrub grows to 1.8–2.4m (6–8ft) high and wide. It has glossy, leathery, oval leaves – turn them over and see the yellowish green undersides. Delight in the late spring light pink or white cup-shaped flowers that have showy stamens resembling stars.

CULTIVATION This shrub needs moist soil that is rich in humus and is acidic. It should be sheltered from drying winds.

HARDINESS Fully hardy/Z5–9

NOTE Look for varieties such as 'Carousel' or 'Kaleidoscope' that have flowers with contrasting colours.

MAINTENANCE Easy. Because *K. l.* is a slow grower, very little pruning will be necessary.

Pieris japonica 'Temple Bells'
ANDROMEDA
FAMILY Ericaceae

This attractive shrub is a slow-growing, dwarf broadleaf evergreen with tiered branches. New foliage emerges as a bronze-apricot colour and over time turns to dark green. Large white flowers in dense drooping clusters appear in late winter or early spring. Grows to 6m (10ft) tall and wide.

CULTIVATION Prefers an acidic, well-drained soil that stays moist – a yearly mulch with pine needles keeps it damp and acidic. Likes cool summers and will become stressed with too much heat.

HARDINESS Fully hardy/Z6–8

ABOVE Sarcococca confusa.

NOTES It is a good choice for containers near entrance ways since it has year-round interest.
MAINTENANCE Easy. Prune by removing spent flowers.

Sarcococca confusa
SWEET BOX
FAMILY Buxaceae

This evergreen shrub is a delight all year, even though its seasonal features are subtle. It's a reliable shade shrub that has a few varieties – some are low growers while the tallest may reach 1.8m (6ft). Ideal for small spaces or grouped as a hedge, this bush has dark, waxy green leaves and tiny white blossoms in late winter. The flowers have a powerful fragrance, which is the main reason for growing this plant. Sweet box grows slowly and keeps an orderly and polished appearance all year.
CULTIVATION A shade lover, this shrub thrives in organically enriched soil.

Growth is slow and orderly, so pruning is rarely needed. Likes moderate water.
HARDINESS Fully hardy/Z6–9
NOTES *S. humilis* is the low-growing variety and can be used as a ground cover. Birds love the berries!
MAINTENANCE Easy. But make sure you weed the seedlings that want to overpopulate the garden.

Styrax japonicus
JAPANESE SNOWBELL
FAMILY Styracaceae

A springtime showpiece, this small deciduous tree may grow to 10m (30ft) and has a slender and graceful trunk. A profusion of white, bell-shaped fragrant flowers hang in clusters, and these later form into fruits that dangle into the autumn.
CULTIVATION Provide good soil that is well drained. This tree has deep-growing roots but they won't take over.
HARDINESS Fully hardy/Z5–9
NOTES Best to plant in a raised bed or on a berm (a mound of earth with sloping sides) where you can look up

into the tree to appreciate the lovely display of white flowers and scallop-edged green leaves. 'Pink Chimes' offers an upright form with pink blossoms.
MAINTENANCE Easy. Prune to keep shape and keep lower branches cut to reduce bushiness.

Taxus cuspidata 'Nana Pyramidalis'
YEW
FAMILY Taxaceae

This slow-growing dark evergreen conifer grows more slowly than most other yews and forms a textured and dense broad pyramidal shape. Dark, thick green foliage is tufted along each stem. Red fruit appears in early autumn. Once established, it is tolerant of shade, coastal conditions, and drought conditions. Reaches a height of 5m (15ft).
CULTIVATION Adaptable to many soil types, but pH levels should not be too alkaline or acidic. It prefers shady areas away from surfaces that radiate heat.
HARDINESS Fully hardy/Z5–7
NOTES This variety is great choice for a privacy screen or a windbreaker. It can be easily sheared to make hedges.
MAINTENANCE Easy. Minimum shearing is needed to maintain its appearance. An excellent choice for a low-maintenance hedge.

BELOW Taxus cuspidata.

VEGETABLES

As we rethink how to garden as we get older, we also need to redefine the concept of a garden and how it might suit our abilities. This is especially true when we plan our vegetable gardens. As the following list illustrates, no matter what your gardening environment, vegetable-growing options are wide. If you are still tending an in-ground vegetable garden, it may be time to cultivate fewer rows, limit the number of varieties you plant and select varieties that are easy to cultivate and harvest. It is always better to have a well-maintained smaller vegetable plot than a large one that can get out of hand.

ABOVE Capsicum *'Santa Fe Grande'* *peppers add great colour and are seen as one of the best varieties for pickling.*

ABOVE Allium cepa *(onion).*

Allium cepa
ONION
FAMILY Amaryllidaceae

There are many varieties of onion – most are round, but some are torpedo-shaped. Golden varieties are good for storing, but reds and whites provide sweeter and milder flavours. Plant the miniature bulbs, called 'sets', in mid- to late spring when the soil is warmer.

CULTIVATION Plant in an open position in rich, well drained, loose soil that has been manured the previous autumn. Since onions are shallow-rooted, they need moisture near the surface.

NOTES Choose an inappropriate variety for your area. Plan them as part of a crop rotation scheme.

MAINTENANCE Moderate.

Beta vulgaris 'Boltardy'
BEETROOT (BEET)
FAMILY Chenopodiaceae

Raised for their edible root, beetroot greens are also a nutritious part of this versatile vegetable.

CULTIVATION Beetroot does well in sun and shade. It likes loose, well-drained soil that is high in organic matter and is not acidic. Remove soil clods or rocks and keep the soil moist. Thrives in almost any climate but where it is hot sow in early spring so that plants mature before the extreme temperatures. Grow as an autumn, late-winter and early-spring crop.

NOTES All beetroot is easy to grow, but 'Boltardy' is the easiest. Use old favourites with round dark maroon roots such as 'Mr Crosby's Egyptian' or 'Detroit Dark Red'. Newer varieties include 'Chioggia' which has rings of red and white. Also tasty vegetables, golden yellow beets are becoming more popular.

MAINTENANCE Moderate. Beetroot does not transplant well, so thin seedlings to 7.5cm (3in) apart and eat the thinned seedlings as you would spinach.

BELOW Beta vulgaris *'Boltardy' (beetroot).*

ABOVE Beta vulgaris *subsp.* cicla *var.* flavescens *(chard).*

Beta vulgaris **subsp.** *cicla* **var.** *flavescens*
RAINBOW CHARD
FAMILY Chenopodiaceae

Part of the beet family, chard is grown for its vitamin-rich leaves.

CULTIVATION Chard tolerates poor soil, inattention, frost and mild freezes. Plant as soon as the soil can be worked – it's an early sprouter. In mild climates, one planting will last the entire year, so plan a permanent place for it.

NOTES Rainbow chard or 'Bright Lights' chard is as beautiful as it is delicious. When the weather starts to cool down, and most other crops are finished for the season, chards of all types will continue to grow. Just cut the leaves as you need them!

MAINTENANCE Easy. Slug-resistant.

Capsicum
PEPPERS
FAMILY Solanaceae

These are attractive bushy plants that grow from 30cm (1ft) to 1.2m (4ft) high. They produce hot and sweet varieties.

CULTIVATION Because peppers are of tropical origin plant them when temperatures are 21–26°C (70–80°F) during the day and 15–21°C (60–70°F) at night. Several weeks before

planting, work the soil 20–25cm (8–10in) deep. The soil should not be sticky. Add ample amounts of organic matter, especially if your soil is heavy. Mulching is crucial for all peppers, especially sweet peppers, because their roots tend to be shallow. Use a material that is slow to break down and will last for the entire season.

NOTES In temperate climates, peppers do best under glass, as they need a long season of warmth to ripen.

MAINTENANCE Moderate. To harvest peppers, snip the stem with secateurs.

Cucumis sativus
CUCUMBER
FAMILY Cucurbitaceae

There are two main types of cucumber: greenhouse varieties and outdoor or ridge varieties. A cucumber vine typically bears small yellow flowers that form into cucumbers. Plants for growing under glass are tall climbing ones that bear long, tasty, slender fruits. Outdoor varieties are bushier in habit, produce shorter fruits and use little space. Shapes vary from the slicing type to the pickling or novelty Asian round variety.

CULTIVATION Wait until warm weather (15–21°C/60–70°F) to plant the seeds. Cucumbers perform best in fertile, well-drained soils in full sun.

BELOW Cucumis sativus *(cucumber).*

ABOVE Cucurbita *'Black Forest' (squash).*

NOTES 'Sweet Success,' 'Fanfare' and 'Lemon' are good bush varieties, suitable for a small garden.

MAINTENANCE Easy. Frequent, shallow cultivation and hand pulling will keep weeds down until the vines cover the ground. Water plants once a week during dry weather.

Cucurbita
SUMMER SQUASH
FAMILY Cucurbitaceae

Squashes can be divided into two main groups: summer and winter types. The former are best used fresh, the latter will store well. Summer squashes come in bush and vine forms; all need plenty of room. Crookneck squashes are a summer type with a long, curved neck. One or two vines of these, if kept under control, will give you an early harvest.

CULTIVATION Cultivate the garden spot until the soil is crumbly and fine, and till in plenty of organic matter.

NOTES Do not water in the evening. Harvest when small and tender. There are numerous varieties of climbing squash, including the summer 'Custard Squash', the summer bush variety 'Tender and True' and the winter 'Turks Turban'.

MAINTENANCE Easy. Give regular moisture, but leaves and stems should be kept as dry as possible.

ABOVE Daucus carota *'Early Nantes'*.

Daucus carota sativus
CARROT
FAMILY Apiaceae

Delicate fern-like green foliage is produced above sweet, tasty roots.
CULTIVATION Prefers light, sandy soil and full sun. Sow the seeds as soon as the ground can be worked and more seeds should be planted every few weeks throughout the summer. The seeds are tiny, which makes sowing them difficult, but you can always use a seed tape or a precision seed sower. If over-seeded, thinning is easily accomplished by snipping off the tops – there is no need to pull.
NOTES Cultivar options are 'Nantes', 'Chantenay', 'Touchon' and 'Short n' Sweet'. Today, various shapes (such as round carrots) and colours such as purple and white are available.
MAINTENANCE Moderate. Avoid irregular watering since dry-to-wet conditions cause the root to split.

Phaseolus vulgaris
FRENCH BEANS, RUNNER BEANS, SNAP BEANS, STRING BEANS
FAMILY Fabaceae

Edible, tender, and fleshy pods grow on self-supporting bushes or climbing vines. Plants have bright green leaves and the flowers are white or purple.

CULTIVATION Plant seeds after the soil reaches 18°C (65°F) and there is no more danger of frost. They like well-drained and fertile soil, which has not recently been planted with beans, potatoes, tomatoes, lettuce or cabbage.
NOTES Bush types are easier to manage, but pole types take up little space and are easier for harvesting. There are many varieties that have both bush and pole growth habits, such as 'Blue Lake', 'Contender' and 'Kentucky Wonder'.
MAINTENANCE Easy. Keep well watered. Harvest when foliage is dry to avoid spreading disease. Rotate crop each year.

Lactuca sativa
LETTUCE
FAMILY Asteraceae

Lettuce comes in four main types: loose-leaf, crisphead, butterhead (Boston) and cos (romaine). The leafy varieties are recommended since they stand the heat better, grow faster and give a longer harvest.

BELOW Lactuca sativa *(lettuce)*.

CULTIVATION Use loose, well-drained soil and barely cover the seeds after sowing. Feed plants lightly and frequently during the growing season. Plant every 2 weeks for prolonged harvests.
NOTES Loose-leaf types come in green and red.
MAINTENANCE Easy. Protect from slugs. To harvest, clip off outer leaves.

Lycopersicon esculentum
TOMATO
FAMILY Solanaceae

Lush and leafy, these plants can be bushy and require little or no staking. Other types are trained as cordons and will need the support of canes or wires.
CULTIVATION Tomatoes require plenty of sun. Set out seedlings after the air and soil have warmed up. They do better if seedlings are planted deeper than they grew in the pot. Plants will be more anchored and sturdier, and roots will develop along the buried portion of the stem. Add compost or manure to the soil.
NOTES Among the best varieties are 'Gardener's Delight', 'Sungold', 'Celebrity', 'Big Rainbow', 'Brandywine' and 'Enchantment'.

ABOVE Lycopersicon esculentum *(tomato).*

MAINTENANCE Moderate. When plants are about 90cm (3ft) tall, remove the leaves from the bottom 2.5cm (1in) of stem to prevent fungus spread. Bush varieties need no training, but for cordons, remove sideshoots as they appear, leaving a single stem, and keep tying it in to the support. Nip out the top when the plant reaches the right height.

Pisum sativum
GREEN SNAP PEAS
FAMILY Leguminosae

Both the bush and climbing varieties that produce shell (shelling) peas, mangetouts (snow peas) and sugarsnap (snap) peas will give a generous harvest despite their delicate appearance.
CULTIVATION Sow seeds early in spring as soon as you can work the soil. Peas love cooler temperate climates and when temperatures exceed 21°C (70°F) most varieties stop producing pods. They grow in most soils but prefer a medium well-dug soil with plenty of organic material. Do not add nitrogen!
NOTES Bush types are easy yet can take up valuable space. Consider climbing or pole types that take up little ground space and are easier for harvesting. Varieties include 'Alderman', 'Sugar Snap', 'Oregon Trail' and 'Super Sugar Mel'.
MAINTENANCE Easy.

Raphanus sativus
RADISH
FAMILY Brassicaceae

A satisfying crop since it germinates quickly and within 2–3 weeks you can be harvesting. Though grown for its root, radish greens are also tasty and nutritious. Most familiar types are the round red or red-and-white varieties. Choose from many varieties that are all white ('White Icicle' or pink ('French Dressing'), or long and narrow. Daikons are radishes that have the hotter flavours.
CULTIVATION Sow seeds during the short, cool days of spring and autumn. During these times, radishes are perhaps the easiest and fastest vegetable to grow. Simply sow seed directly into the soil. As you harvest a row, plant another and enjoy radishes all spring and summer long.
NOTES Varieties include 'Cherry Belle', 'White Icicle' and 'Scarlet Globe'.
MAINTENANCE Easy.

Solanum tuberosum
POTATOES
FAMILY Solanaceae

Potatoes are undoubtedly one of the most popular vegetables. The foliage part of a potato is an attractive small bush of divided dark green

BELOW Raphanus sativus *(radish).*

ABOVE Solanum tuberosum *(potatoes).*

leaves that in time are companions for the star-shaped, clustered, pale-blue flowers.
CULTIVATION You need to 'chit' the seed potatoes by arranging them, with the 'eyes' facing up, in the light in a cool but frost-free room. They are ready for planting when the sprouts have reached 2cm (¾in) in length, which will take approximately 4–6 weeks. Before planting, loosen up the soil 20–30cm (8–12in) deep and mix in some compost – leaf mould is also a good option. It is best to plant in moist but not sodden soil. Plant no earlier than 2 weeks before your last frost with a soil temperature above 7°C (45°F). Cut the seed potato into egg-sized pieces, leaving one or more 'eyes' on each.
NOTES If an in-ground garden bed is not available or too low for you to tend comfortably, potatoes can be grown easily and abundantly in large 75-litre (20-gallon) containers or bags. Keep near your kitchen and you can have fresh potatoes when they are in season.
MAINTENANCE Easy. Always make sure that developing tubers are covered with soil to keep skin from turning green (this can be toxic to eat).

FRUIT

One of the advantages of being a senior is that we remember how fruit is supposed to taste! Growing your own guarantees that you'll have fresh and flavourful fruit that will delight your taste buds. The varieties listed here require fairly low care and maintenance, often take little space to grow, and some will thrive in containers. To lengthen your berry harvests, take note of the early, mid, and late ripening options. Finally, even gardens with limited space can be home to at least one fruit tree since new breeding has created varieties that are compact and columnar shaped. Always choose fruits that you enjoy eating.

ABOVE *Blueberries, strawberries and raspberries brighten up your garden and can then be harvested for use.*

ABOVE Cucumis melo *'Iroquois' (cantaloupe melon).*

Cucumis melo
CANTALOUPE MELON
FAMILY **Cucurbitaceae**
This delicious fruiting annual has trailing, soft, hairy vines that can cover a good deal of ground. The small rounded fruit has a 'netted' skin pattern with the edible flesh varying from light green to reddish orange.
CULTIVATION Melons prefer fertile, humus-rich, well-drained, sandy soils. Warm-season crops, cantaloupes should be planted when all danger of frost has passed. The ideal climate consists of a long, frost-free season with plenty of sunshine and heat, and relatively low humidity. Plant in the spring when the soil temperature is 18–29°C (65–85°F).

NOTES In areas with a short growing season, use transplants to get a head start. Cantaloupe can be trained to a fence, trellis or grown in a large pot. As the fruit grows, support it with cloth slings since the weight may damage the vines.
MAINTENANCE Moderate. Look for varieties resistant to mildew and other diseases. 'Ambrosia', 'Classic Hybrid', 'Hales Best', 'Mission', 'Rocky Sweet' and 'Summit Hybrid' are all excellent.

Ficus carica
FIG
FAMILY **Moraceae**
CULTIVATION Figs thrive in a spot with full sun, preferably near a sunny wall. They are not fussy about soil, but give them space. They appreciate regular water and excellent drainage. Figs do not need other varieties for pollination.
NOTES Fig trees will grow quite large before producing good crops, unless the roots are restricted. They are traditionally planted in 60cm (2ft) deep and wide pits, with paving stones forming the sides and broken bricks or stones at the bottom. 'Brown Turkey' is a reliable variety and 'Negronne' is a dwarf variety which grows to only 1.8m (6ft) high.
MAINTENANCE Easy. Figs are best planted when dormant – in autumn and winter. They need only minimal pruning. Protect fruit from birds by using netting.

BELOW Ficus carica *(fig).*

Fragaria x *ananassa*
STRAWBERRY
FAMILY Rosaceae
These low growers, which are 1.8–2.4m (6–8ft) tall, have toothy, roundish leaves and white flowers. They spread by runners to about 30cm (1ft) long.

CULTIVATION These plants like well-drained and acidic soil. Grow in full sun or bright partial shade. When planting, hill the centre of the hole and position the crown of the plant at soil level. Spread the roots down the slope and cover with soil so that it reaches just halfway up the crown. Plants need regular moisture during the fruiting season. In the winter, mulch with a layer of straw or other weed-free light organic material. Strawberries grow well with bush beans, spinach, borage and lettuce.

NOTES Buy your plants from local suppliers using types that do well in your climate. Strawberries will thrive in containers where the soil and drainage conditions can be controlled.

MAINTENANCE Easy. If you cut off the runner plants early you will encourage larger fruit. Use straw or pine-needle mulch between rows in spring to keep the ground moist and the fruit clean.

Fortunella margarita
KUMQUAT
FAMILY Rutaceae
Kumquats have been called 'the little gems of the citrus family'. Shrub types grow 1.8–4.5m (6–15ft) while dwarf versions reach only 90cm–1.8m (3–6ft), ideal for a small garden. They are slow growing with thornless branches that are light green and angled when young. The lance-shaped leaves are a glossy dark green. Sweetly fragrant white flowers appear and then form small oval fruits with golden-yellow to reddish-orange peel.

CULTIVATION Kumquats are among the most cold-hardy citrus trees on earth. They love climates where the summer days are hot but the nights are chilly.

ABOVE Fortunella japonica *(kumquats)*.

They grow reliably in most types of soil, but prefer a sandy loam.

NOTES The kumquat has a thin, sweet peel and a zesty, somewhat tart centre. Eat kumquats unpeeled, as you would eat grapes. They taste best if you roll them between your fingers first as this releases the essential oils in the rind. Another tasty variety is *F. japonica*.

MAINTENANCE Easy. Needs very little pruning, just a little for shaping. Each year apply a few doses of nitrogen fertilizer such as fish emulsion. Whenever the temperature drops to 4°C (24°F) or below try to protect the fruit by wrapping it in hessian (burlap), or if it is in a container, move it to a sheltered spot.

BELOW Fragaria x ananassa *'Calypso' (strawberries)*.

Malus sylvestris var. *domestica*
COLUMNAR APPLE TREE
FAMILY Rosaceae

Many gardens do not have the space to grow full-size apple trees so a new type of apple tree has been created, the columnar. Mature trees average 2.4–3m (8–10ft) tall and only about 60cm (2ft) wide. They can grow and produce healthy fruit for about 20 years.

CULTIVATION Plant in full sun and provide good, well-drained soil. In cold climates container-grown trees will need winter protection.

NOTES They work well as potted plants, making them portable. Early producers, they may grow fruit on their first year. 'Northpole' and 'Golden Sentinel' resemble Golden Delicious in taste.

MAINTENANCE Easy.

Prunus cerasus
SOUR CHERRY TREE
FAMILY Rosaceae

These small cherry trees grow from 4.5–7.5m (15–25ft) tall. Their compact size allows for easy maintenance and harvest. Many produce a mouth-watering crop of plump, juicy fruit that ripens in midsummer. They are dependably hardy, with huge harvests for pies and preserves. These trees are self-pollinating so you do not need multiples for successful pollination.

CULTIVATION Like full sun. Avoid heavy clay and wet soils – they prefer rich, well-drained, moist soils. Do not soak for over 24 hours prior to planting.

NOTES The 'North Star' variety produces full size fruit even though it grows only 1.8–2.4m (6–8ft). The sour fruit has light red skin, perfect for pies and pastries.

MAINTENANCE Easy. To avoid disease do any pruning in the summer and not during the usual cool dormancy months. They need more nitrogen and water than sweet cherries so use a slow-release fertilizer high in nitrogen.

Pyrus serotina
ASIAN PEAR TREE
FAMILY Rosaceae

This is an excellent ornamental espalier or deciduous shade tree. In spring it's covered with white blossoms and the glossy attractive leaves are tinged with purple all summer and into autumn. It can reach 7.5–9m (25–30ft) high and 4.5m (15ft) wide.

BELOW Prunus incisa *'Oshidori'*
(dwarf cherry tree).

ABOVE Rubus idaeus.

CULTIVATION Grow in full sun in deep well-drained soil. Trees can tolerate heavy wet soils. Ripening happens from late summer to autumn.

NOTES Asian pears are sometimes called apple pears because they are round like apples but juicier and with a different texture. Unlike most European pears, the fruit ripens on the tree. Another variety of Asian pear is *Pyrus pyrifolia*.

MAINTENANCE Moderate. With prudent pruning, tree size can be reduced to half. Thin fruit to one pear per cluster to have larger fruit.

Rubus idaeus
RASPBERRY
FAMILY Rosaceae

Raspberries may be red, black, purple or yellow-fruited. There are summer-fruiting types, which crop once in midsummer, and autumn-fruiting (ever-bearing), which fruit continuously from late summer to the first frosts (or, in hot climates, may produce an early and a late crop).

CULTIVATION Raspberries do best in full sun but will tolerate slight shade.

NOTES Apply a general all-purpose fertilizer in late winter, one that is low in nitrogen since too much of it can result in bushy plants and less berries.

MAINTENANCE Moderate. Fruited canes should be cut down after fruiting, and autumn varieties trimmed again in spring. The most common disease is fungus so keep the plants thinned to allow air circulation. Insects are not a common problem. Plants will need replacing every 7–8 years, as they are often weakened by viruses and lose productivity.

Ribes nigrum
BLACKCURRANT
FAMILY Grossulariaceae

Currant bushes are deciduous and fast growing under optimum conditions. They grow a multiple-stemmed clump, up to 1.5m (5ft) high and wide, but can be pruned for shape. Blackcurrant leaves are pale green, while those of the red currant are deep blue-green.

CULTIVATION Currants like morning sun and afternoon part-shade with ample air circulation. Intense sunlight will scorch leaves. Frequent cultivation will damage the shallow and superficial roots, so keep them well mulched. Water until harvest.

BELOW Ribes nigrum *'Ben Sarek'* *(blackcurrant bush).*

ABOVE Ribes uvacrispa *(gooseberries).*

NOTES Plants are thornless and fruits are small (pea-sized), produced and harvested in a grape-like cluster called a 'strig'.

MAINTENANCE Moderate. They need protection against various pests, including birds.

Ribes uvacrispa
GOOSEBERRY
FAMILY Grossulariaceae

This multi-stemmed bush grows between 90cm–1.5m (3–5ft) tall and wide, and produces translucent, round, green berries with stripes. The leaves resemble those of a maple and give a lovely autumn colour.

CULTIVATION These cold hardy plants prefer cool, moist, well-drained sites. Plant in a medium-weight soil that is well drained but not dry. If the fruit is to develop fully, moisture is required. However, in very fertile soil, the plant produces too much green growth at the expense of good fruit.

NOTES Gooseberries make jams, jellies, preserves and pies, and some are sweet enough to eat raw when ripe. 'Pixwell' is hardy and almost thornless.

MAINTENANCE Easy. To prevent fungal disease, select planting sites with good air movement.

Rubus spp.
BLACKBERRY
FAMILY Rosaceae

The berry varieties suggested here are thornless, self-supporting canes. The firm berries are conical and are bright glossy black. The leaves usually have three or five oval coarsely toothed, stalked leaflets.

CULTIVATION Blackberries grow best in fertile and well-drained soils that get regular moisture throughout the growing season. Fruit will ripen best in hot summer.

NOTES Disease-resistant blackberry varieties include 'Ouachita', 'Navaho' and 'Arapaho'. Other popular varieties are the easy growing, thornless 'Loch Ness', the flavoursome 'Fantasia' and the large, delicious fruits of 'Sylvan'. Plants are vigorous so need sturdy supports. Watch out for thorns.

MAINTENANCE Moderate. Fertilize at bloom time with a food high in nitrogen.

Vaccinium corymbosum
BLUEBERRIES
FAMILY Ericaceae

While grown for the fruit, blueberry bushes make handsome hedges and borders. They give visual interest nearly all year round as white or pink urn-shaped flowers appear in spring, and then spectacular autumnal leaf displays.

CULTIVATION Blueberries prefer full sun and a very acid soil. Buy several plants so you can benefit from blueberries from early summer right through to late autumn.

NOTE If your soil is neutral or alkaline, grow blueberries in containers but keep them well watered at all times.

MAINTENANCE Moderate. Water regularly in the spring and summer and use rainwater whenever possible. Use an ericaceous (azalea/camellia-formulated) fertilizer when spring growth begins, and again after harvest. Prune old growth to encourage younger branches.

HERBS

Herbs have an established history as garden plants and are still used for their medicinal properties, their flavours and their scents. Most herbs are small flowering plants. In many cases it is the leaves of the herbs that are used, but sometimes it is the flowers or the stem or root. The following list introduces a selection that will give a garden varied colours, textures and growth habits. Many have an important role in providing food for birds and butterflies. All those included here have the potential to tantalize the senses of smell, touch, sight and taste. They are all easy to grow and need minimum care.

ABOVE Lavandula angustifolia *is all that a plant should be: fragrant, beautiful, fast-growing and irresistible to bees.*

Allium schoenoprasum
CHIVES
FAMILY **Alliaceae**
Closely related to the onion and garlic, and also to the many ornamental alliums, this clumping plant has hollow tubular grass-like leaves that are flavourful in salads. In late spring, light purple flowers appear on 30cm (12in) stalks.
CULTIVATION Provide an open, sunny situation and free-draining soil. Grows well if left undisturbed for several years to form large clumps. Easily propagated by seed in autumn, or by dividing the clumps in spring.
HARDINESS Fully hardy/Z3–9

NOTES Chives can be grown inside or out. Also a great companion plant: a large area of chives planted under roses will help to ward off blackspot.
MAINTENANCE Easy.

Foeniculum vulgare
FENNEL
FAMILY **Apiaceae**
This handsome perennial will add grace, height and airy texture. With bright green, finely fern-like leaves and aromatic yellow flowers, plant fennel in the back of the herb or perennial flower garden as it will grow to 2m (6ft) tall.

BELOW Foeniculum vulgare.

CULTIVATION The plants require full sunlight and well-drained, deep, moderately fertile soil. Best planted in a more spacious garden where architectural structure may be needed.
HARDINESS Fully hardy/Z4–9
NOTES Fennel attracts bees, butterflies and birds. All parts of the plant are edible – the leaves, stems, seeds and roots. The plants release a chemical that inhibits the growth of some other plants, so do not plant very close to beans, tomatoes or cabbage family plants.
MAINTENANCE Easy. It seeds freely so new seedlings will require weeding to control their spread.

Lavandula angustifolia
LAVENDER
FAMILY **Lamiaceae**
One of the most popular herbs, lavender plants can be a small shrub reaching up to 90cm (3ft) in height. It provides fragrance, beauty, and there are many uses for its grey-green leaves and spikes of purple/lavender flowers.
CULTIVATION Likes well-drained soil with abundant sun. It is best propagated by cuttings. If winters are severe, some varieties will need protection.
HARDINESS Fully hardy/Z6–9
NOTES The 'Hidcote' variety works well along paths, as it is erect and has a neat habit. 'Munstead' is ideal in containers. The French cultivar

'Grosso' is a heavy bloomer, with flowers that have a strong fragrance. When dried, the flowering stems make excellent everlasting bouquets and have uses in many crafts.
MAINTENANCE Easy. Cut back after flowering is over.

Mentha spicata
SPEARMINT
FAMILY Lamiaceae
This is the most popular culinary mint because of its wonderful flavour and scent. It is a crisp-looking plant with pointed crinkly leaves and purple flowers in the summer.
CULTIVATION Like most mint plants, this one likes full sun and rich, moist soil. Because of its tendency to become invasive, grow mint in a bottomless container that is buried in the garden bed to contain its spread.
HARDINESS Fully to frost hardy/Z5–9
NOTES Grow spearmint near an outside doorway (in a container works well) – then, on a hot day you will benefit from its refreshing scent wafting through the air. Blossoms attract bees, butterflies and other beneficial insects.

BELOW Mentha spicata.

ABOVE Monarda didyma 'Garden View'.

The birds like to feast on the seed heads so leave some for their autumn-time forage. Dry the leaves just before flowering for future use.
MAINTENANCE Easy.

Monarda didyma
BEE-BALM, BERGAMOT
FAMILY Lamiaceae
This handsome perennial is a dramatic filler where height is needed in a bed. The 1.2m (4ft) stems rise from strong clumps and form spiky scarlet blossoms and a welcome splash of colour and texture. The lemon-scented leaves resemble those of mint.
CULTIVATION Plant bee-balm in full sun in a well-drained soil that retains some moisture. A good mulching helps since the plant is not drought tolerant. Divide to propagate.
HARDINESS Fully hardy/Z4–8
NOTES This vintage plant will attract bees, hummingbirds and butterflies, as well as other beneficial insects to your garden.
MAINTENANCE Look for varieties that are resistant to mildew. With vigilant deadheading, you can have flowers for eight weeks or more.

Nepeta x *faassenii*
CATMINT
FAMILY Lamiaceae
This member of the mint family is not invasive. Its soft silvery grey-green heart-shaped foliage grows on graceful thin twigs. It grows 45cm (18in) high and wide and spikes of lavender flowers appear from late spring to summer.
CULTIVATION Catmint is happiest in a well-drained soil in full sun. While drought tolerant, in hot climates it appreciates some afternoon shade. It has a moderate need for water. Rock gardens are perfect settings for catmint, as are border fronts, herb gardens or naturalized plantings.
HARDINESS Fully hardy/Z4–8
NOTES The leaves of this hybrid are fragrant and less attractive to cats than some species. The blooms are useful as fillers in bouquets. Butterflies and hummingbirds are attracted to their nectar, but deer and rabbits are repelled by mint-scented foliage. 'Walker's Low' is a lovely variety.
MAINTENANCE Easy. No serious insect or disease problems. Shear flower spikes after initial flowering to promote a continuous blooming.

BELOW Nepeta x faassenii.

Ocimum basilicum
SWEET BASIL
FAMILY Lamiaceae

One of the most popular herbs, sweet basil is an annual that thrives in warm temperatures. The tender green leaves grow on stalks.

CULTIVATION An easy plant to grow from seed. When the plant is 10–15cm (4–6in) pinch back the tips to encourage new growth and remove the flowers to ensure the leaves continue to grow.

HARDINESS Frost tender/Z8

NOTES 'Dark Opal' has large, bronzy purple leaves and is a great addition to borders, planted among other ornamentals.

MAINTENANCE Easy. All you need to do is prevent the basil from flowering so you have a longer harvest of tasty leaves.

Origanum vulgare
OREGANO, WILD MARJORAM
FAMILY Lamiaceae

An upright-growing herb with square stems and broad, oval-shaped green leaves. In summer white flower clusters are borne, which bees love. Can reach 45cm (18in).

CULTIVATION Oregano likes full sun and poor to moderately fertile, well-drained soil. The best ways to propagate are by planting seeds or taking tip cuttings.

HARDINESS Fully hardy/Z4–8

NOTES To keep the flavour, prune off most of the flowers – but let a few stay to attract the pollinators such as bees and butterflies.

MAINTENANCE Easy.

BELOW Origanum vulgare.

ABOVE Petroselinum crispum.

Petroselinum crispum
PARSLEY
FAMILY Apiaceae

The world's most popular herb, parsley, is widely known as the limp green garnish on our dinner plates. But this tightly curled balm-scented dark-green leaf plant can enhance a garden border, flowerbed or container with appealing texture and substance.

CULTIVATION Parsley needs a good amount of light and will do best when it gets around 6 hours of sun. It will also tolerate partial shade. It likes a well-drained, moisture-retaining, fertile, humus-rich soil. (If you grow it in containers do ensure there are adequate drainage holes.) Set out transplants from the nursery after the last risk of frost.

HARDINESS Half hardy/Z4–9

NOTES Parsley leaves can be cut all season long. You can continue cutting all winter if you have it in pots under glass; the leaves can be dried, but have little flavour. Parsley attracts many beneficial creatures such as lady beetles, green lacewings, spiders and hoverflies; all use the parsley flower as a safe landing site and an egg repository.

MAINTENANCE Easy. Parsley can overwinter if it is lightly mulched during extremely cold weather. Remove the flower stems when they appear – this will keep the plants producing leaves.

Rosmarinus officinalis
ROSEMARY
FAMILY Lamiaceae

This frost-hardy evergreen perennial blooms from mid-spring to early summer, and often again in autumn. Upright varieties reach a height of 90cm–1.8m (3–6ft) and low trailing types do very well in containers. It has narrow, highly fragrant leaves and abundant pale blue flowers.

CULTIVATION Grows best in sun and in well-drained soil. Place in a sheltered location. Propagates easily from cuttings. Grows well in containers.

HARDINESS Frost hardy/Z7–9

NOTES Though not fully hardy, it can survive down to -10°C (14°F) in well-drained soil. Fresh leaves can be cut at any time for culinary use. To dry leaves it is best to take cuttings just before the plant blooms.

MAINTENANCE Easy.

Salvia elegans
PINEAPPLE SAGE
FAMILY Lamiaceae

This impressive perennial grows upright to a height and width of 90–120cm (3–4ft) and has bright green leaves with a strong aroma of ripe

BELOW Rosmarinus officinalis.

ABOVE Salvia elegans.

pineapple. In mild areas, it blooms from autumn to spring, showcasing bright red delicate tubular flowers. Hummingbirds love this herb.

CULTIVATION Salvia loves full sun, good air circulation to deter mildew and moist but well-drained, humus-rich, modestly fertile soil. Good soil drainage helps keep the plant from waterlogging and having roots that freeze in winter. Easy to propagate from cuttings or seeds or dividing the roots.

HARDINESS Frost hardy/Z8–10

NOTES 'Scarlet Pineapple' grows to 90–120cm (3–4ft). The hybrid 'Frieda Dixon' can be used as a ground cover.

MAINTENANCE Easy. Tall varieties, if grown in part shade, will need staking.

Salvia officinalis
COMMON SAGE
FAMILY Lamiaceae

This shrubby perennial has oval, grey-green, velvety leaves – these are aromatic and the plant is frequently used as a culinary herb. In late spring and summer lavender blue flower spikes emerge. Many colourful varieties are available from variegated leaves to those

blushing with red violet. Grows 30–90cm (1–3ft) tall and 30–60cm (1–2ft) wide.

CULTIVATION The same as S. elegans (see previous entry).

HARDINESS Half hardy/Z6–9

NOTES Salvias are part of the mint family and are the largest genus in this group. Attracts birds, bees and butterflies.

MAINTENANCE Moderate. Prune in winter or early spring when temperatures are cool and new growth is emerging. After flowering, keep shaped by tip-pinching.

Thymus vulgaris
THYME
FAMILY *Lamiaceae*

This commonly grown shrubby herb offers highly flavoured leaves and lilac flowers that are borne in small clusters. Grows to about 30cm (1ft).

CULTIVATION Grows best in a sunny position in light, well-drained soil. It works well as an edging plant or for a spreading growth over rocks.

HARDINESS Hardy/Z7

NOTES T. serpyllum, creeping thyme, reaches only 25cm (10in), a great choice for containers or a filler between paving stones. T. x citriodorus is a lemon-scented variety.

MAINTENANCE Easy.

BELOW Thymus serpyllum.

INDOOR PLANTS

For those who have downsized or have become too frail to work outdoors, growing indoor plants provides an invaluable opportunity for continuing to garden within your own four walls. These plants are dependent on you for regular care, and caring for natural living things promotes a rewarding sense of stewardship. Houseplants are known to reduce stress and improve psychological well-being and physical health, since many plants remove toxins, pollutants and carbon dioxide from our air. This list of plants should give you a head start in selecting the right plant for your environment and energy levels.

ABOVE *Begonias are easy and much-loved houseplants. They are equally prized for their flowers as for their showy leaves.*

Aechmea fasciata
BROMELIAD
FAMILY **Bromeliaceae**

Part of a distinct plant family, in the wild these plants are considered 'air plants' since they grow on trees and shrubs using their leaves as water and food absorbers. However, they are easy to grow indoors and will provide you with beautiful forms, foliage, and flowers that grow up to 60cm (2ft) tall and can last for 3 months. The 'tank bromeliad' forms a tight clumped rosette of sturdy leaves that encircle a small reservoir cup.

CULTIVATION Pot in shallow containers using an orchid potting mixture or one

that provides good drainage. Keep some water in the reservoir cup at all times and make sure the potting medium is moist. They like bright light. Frequent mistings keeps the foliage clean and healthy.

NOTES The pineapple is one of the most familiar bromeliads. 'Silver Urn' is a very popular variety and a good beginner bromeliad with dark green leaves with silvery bands and a beautiful pink inflorescence.

MAINTENANCE Easy. Generally free of pest and disease problems.

Aglaonema
CHINESE EVERGREEN
FAMILY **Araceae**

This upright plant has subtly patterned greyish green, waxy, lance-shaped leaves that rise from a central growth. They may get to 90cm (3ft) tall and are grown for their handsome foliage as well as the spathe-shaped flower.

CULTIVATION Grow in a low light and avoid draughts or cold temperatures. They enjoy the same indoor temperature as you. For extra humidity, stand them on trays of damp pebbles. Water to keep soil moist, but between waterings let the top 2.5cm (1in) dry out.

NOTES *A. modestum* 'Silver Queen' has foliage that is silvery green with some dark green, or the reverse, mostly

LEFT **Aglaonema modestum.**

dark green with light green streaks.

MAINTENANCE Easy, but keep temperature above 12°C (55°F). Leaves may be toxic to pets and children so take care where you place it.

Begonia boweri
EYELASH BEGONIA
FAMILY **Begoniaceae**

Appreciated for its foliage, this gets its nickname 'eyelash begonia' from the hairs on the leaf margins. Grows to a height of 15–30cm (6–12in).

CULTIVATION These like filtered light and can tolerate shade. Give them a minimum night temperature of 15–18°C (60–65°F). They like a light, well-drained, soil-less or loam-based compost (soil mix). Keep the soil uniformly moist, but not wet. Fertilize once a month with a balanced fertilizer.

NOTES Propagate by dividing the rhizomes, or from leaf cuttings.

MAINTENANCE Easy.

Begonia rex
REX BEGONIA
FAMILY **Begoaniaceae**

This begonia species is the most striking with colourful patterns on the foliage. Tiny flowers on tall stems are overshadowed by lush leaves. Plants reach 30–45cm (12–18in) tall.

CULTIVATION Enjoys warm and moist conditions with indirect sun. Plant in loamy soil and keep soil dry in winter.

ABOVE Chlorophytum comosum.

NOTES They like a light, well-drained, soil-less or loam-based compost (potting mix).

MAINTENANCE Moderate. Mist daily.

Chlorophytum comosum
SPIDER PLANT
FAMILY Liliaceae

Spider plants just keep on giving. The foliage grows in clumps of soft drooping leaves, usually green or green and white, that have the appearance of long blades of grass. It reaches 15–20cm (6–8in) high and 15–30cm (6–12in) wide. Tiny white flowers are borne on long stalks, and plantlets are produced on attractive, hanging runners. Baby spider plants will normally appear frequently, but if you want to encourage more babies then keep the mother plant in a darkened room.

CULTIVATION It grows best in bright light but will survive with lower light levels. While best to keep it away from midday sun, it is tolerant of a variety of temperatures. When dangling babies start to form roots, they can be cut off and planted on their own.

NOTES Spider plants are believed to be among the most effective for removing toxins from the air.

MAINTENANCE Easy. Repotting may be necessary every couple of years. Brown tips are an indication of the soil being too dry and a feeding prompt.

Davallia fejeensis
RABBIT'S-FOOT FERN, SQUIRREL'S-FOOT FERN
FAMILY Polypodiaceae

This unusual fern has its delicate fronds rising from woolly-textured rhizomes – which are said to look like rabbits' feet. A perfect plant for a wire hanging basket since this container allows you to see both the furry feet and the delicate, airy and lacy fronds. Can reach 90cm (3ft).

CULTIVATION The rabbit's-foot fern likes to be near a bright window. Can tolerate cool temperatures without damage. Keep soil moist but not soggy. To propagate, separate a fuzzy rhizome with at least three fronds and plant in potting mixture. Loves humidity so mist daily and place on a tray of moist pebbles.

NOTES When repotting, plant rhizomes shallowly since they do not like to be covered with soil.

MAINTENANCE Moderate. Keep them well misted and moist.

Epipremnum aureum
POTHOS
FAMILY Araceae

Pothos will commonly trail beyond a distance of 3m (10ft). Leathery dark green leaves 5–10cm (2–4in) long are pointed and oval. Pruning them regularly keeps the plants full at the base.

CULTIVATION Pothos like to grow in a good light but can tolerate shade. Give them rich, loose, well-drained soil. Let the plant dry out between waterings. You can let them trail down or secure

them to a support or trellis. Each cutting can be rooted in water to create more plants.

NOTES There are many variegated and golden varieties available. Look for the golden 'Devil's Ivy' or the white and pale green flecked 'Marble Queen'.

MAINTENANCE Very easy. Sometimes the leaves need a dusting.

Fatsia japonica
JAPANESE ARALIA
FAMILY Araliaceae (ginseng family)

This dramatic plant has large glossy leaves up to 40cm (16in) wide. They are deeply lobed and slightly serrated. Flowers are white, held on a white stalk in small terminal clusters. Height ranges from 90–180cm (3–6ft). During the growing season, provide a monthly feeding of a complete organic fertilizer.

CULTIVATION Grows best in moist, acid, humus-rich soils. Likes part sun and can tolerate shade. Water when soil surface feels dry.

NOTES Can be grown outdoors during summers in temperate climates.

MAINTENANCE Easy, seldom bothered by pests or disease. If leaves turn yellow, supplement with iron.

RIGHT Epipremnum aureum.

ABOVE Phalaenopsis spp.

ABOVE Streptocarpus x hybrid.

ABOVE Saintpaulia ionantha.

Peperomia spp.
PEPEROMIA
FAMILY **Piperaceae**

A low-growing houseplant, the peperomia comes in diverse sizes (up to 25cm/10in), shapes and textures. The thick, fleshy, heart-shaped leaves often have attractive silvery variegations, and they produce unusual white or green flowers that resemble long, rounded or pointed sticks.

CULTIVATION These need to be shaded from the hot sun, but they like bright, indirect sunlight. Room temperatures of at least 12.5°C (55°F) will do, but they appreciate more warmth and good humidity. They do well in small or shallow pots.

NOTES The occasional pinching out of growing points will induce plants to produce more side-shoots and to become bushier. Houseplant favourites include *P.* 'Amigo Greensplit', which has leaves like bean pods, and the variegated succulent, *P. obtusifolia.*

MAINTENANCE Moderate. Water sparingly and always dry completely before watering, especially in the winter months.

Phalaenopsis spp.
MOTH ORCHID
FAMILY **Orchidaceae**

Moth orchids produce alternate wide, fleshy leaves, often marbled in silver with no visible stem. They are epiphytic, often growing on tree branches in the wild (though not parasitic), with aerial roots. The flower stalk is long and arching (up to 60cm/2ft tall) and bears up to 30 large flowers in white to purple shades. Each flower will last a month or more.

CULTIVATION Requires bright indirect light and high humidity. Use orchid compost, in a special orchid basket or transparent pot. When watering, drench it and let it dry out. Set plants on trays of gravel partly filled with water. During the warmer months mist them every day or two. In the autumn, cool night-time temperatures encourage flower spikes. Once these have developed, maintain a constant temperature, 20–21°C (68–70°F), since swings in heat can hurt blooms.

NOTES When the last flower fades, look at the spike for small, fleshy nodes and count out 3 from the base (ignore any that are dried out). Cut the spike 2.5cm (1in) above the third node.

MAINTENANCE Moderate. Fertilize twice a month with a weak fertilizer in the growing season, and water sparingly in winter. Check regularly for insect pests.

Pilea cadierei
ALUMINIUM PLANT
FAMILY **Urticaceae**

This fast-growing plant with watery stems gets it name from the silvery leaf markings on its pointed, oval leaves. Ideally suited for windowsills and tables, it can grow to 30cm (1ft).

CULTIVATION Does best in bright to filtered light. Keep the soil barely moist. Use an all-purpose potting soil.

MAINTENANCE Easy. If it becomes straggly, start new plants from cuttings or by dividing or detaching rosettes.

Plectranthus australis
SWEDISH IVY
FAMILY **Lamiaceae**

Not a true ivy, this plant is related to the mint family. Its leathery leaves are glossy green with crenate leaf edges. It is a fast-growing, trailing plant with spiky white flowers.

CULTIVATION Allow soil to dry slightly between waterings. Likes bright, indirect light. Pinch back to promote full growth.
NOTES Many types have a distinctive odour when touched.
MAINTENANCE Easy.

Saintpaulia ionantha
AFRICAN VIOLET
FAMILY **Gesneriaceae**
At the base of this flowering plant forms a rosette of green, velvet-like, round or pointed leaves from which emerge small, five-petalled flowers that come in many shapes and shades.
CULTIVATION Grow in medium light, ideally a bright, east window. Twelve hours or more light will improve flowering. Requires a moisture-retentive soil medium that is fast-draining. Water with room-tepid water from above or below, but avoid getting water on the leaves which causes spotting. Let it dry out between waterings.
NOTES It dislikes draughts and temperature changes, but if happy will flower for long periods.
MAINTENANCE Easy. Propagate from leaf cuttings or divisions. If mealybugs appear, dip a swab in rubbing alcohol and wipe off, repeating as necessary.

BELOW Schlumbergera *x* buckleyi.

Schlumbergera x *buckleyi*
CHRISTMAS CACTUS
FAMILY **Cactaceae**
Also called 'leaf cactus', this trailing cactus produces deep pink or red flowers in early winter. Can reach 60cm (2ft).
CULTIVATION Keep soil moist during the growing season and dry during dormancy. Can survive a low light, but you'll get more flowers in bright light.
NOTES Force your Christmas cactus to bloom in December (in the Northern Hemisphere) by keeping it in complete darkness for 12 hours a night, starting in mid-October, until buds appear.
MAINTENANCE Moderate. Feed every 2 weeks with balanced liquid fertilizer until blooms drop. Prune after blooming, if necessary.

Spathyphyluum wallisii
PEACE LILY
FAMILY **Araceae**
Favoured for its smooth, glossy, lance-shaped leaves, this is a great addition to a low-lit room. It is fun to watch a new leaf emerge as it unfolds from a sheathed stalk. In spring – and, if you are lucky, in the autumn – the spiky, cream-coloured flowers appear surrounded by white hoods (called spathes).
CULTIVATION Peace lilies like to be grown in medium or low light – direct sunlight will burn the foliage. Sensitive to dry air, they should be well-misted or placed on a tray of moist pebbles. Rarely grows higher than 65cm (26in).
NOTES To extend the blooming time, try to keep water off the flowers. Look for larger varieties, like 'Mauna Loa'.
MAINTENANCE Very easy. Considered one of the healthiest indoor plants.

Streptocarpus hybrids
STREPTOCARPUS
FAMILY **Gesneriaceae**
This robust bloomer has a rosette-forming base with coarse, crinkled, dark green, primrose-like leaves, 15–35cm

ABOVE Tolmiea menziesii.

(6–14in) long. Thin, tall flower stalks grow up from the base. Each plant bears between two and six pale-pink to dark-blue trumpet-shaped flowers. Often flowers stay all year round.
CULTIVATION Grow in bright light but not direct sunlight. They do well in warm room temperatures and need additional humidity in hotter environments. Water moderately, allowing the top half of the soil to dry out.
NOTES *S.* 'Constant Nymph' is a popular hybrid, with blue flowers.
MAINTENANCE Easy.

Tolmiea menziesii
PIGGY BACK PLANT
FAMILY **Saxifragaceae**
Has medium to dark green, hairy leaves, roughly heart-shaped with deeply lobed edges. The leaves are also deeply veined. Each leaf bears a live, young plant appearing in the axil where the leaf meets the short leaf stem. The plant can reach a height of nearly 30cm (1ft).
CULTIVATION Grow in bright light but not direct sunlight. Does well in warmer temperatures and needs additional humidity in hotter environments. Water moderately, allowing the top half of the soil to dry out.
MAINTENANCE Easy.

INDEX

PLANT HARDINESS ZONES

Plant entries in the directory of this book have been given hardiness descriptions and zone numbers. Hardiness definitions are as follows:

Frost tender
A plant needing heated greenhouse protection through the winter in the local area. May be damaged by temperatures below 5°C (41°F).

Half hardy
A plant which cannot be grown outside during the colder months in the local area and needs greenhouse protection through the winter. Can withstand temperatures down to 0°C (32°F).

Frost hardy
A plant which, when outside, survives through milder winters in the local area, with additional protection. Withstands temperatures down to –5°C (23°F).

Fully hardy
A plant which, when planted outside, survives reliably through the winter in the local area. Can withstand temperatures down to –15°C (5°F).

There is widespread use of the zone number system to express the hardiness of many plant species and cultivars. The zonal system used, shown below, was developed by the Agricultural Research Service of the United States Department of Agriculture. According to this system, there are 11 zones in total, based on the average annual minimum temperature in a particular geographical zone.

Each plant's zone rating indicates the coldest zone in which a correctly planted subject can survive the winter. Where hardiness is borderline, the first number shows the marginal zone and the second the safer zone.

This is not a hard and fast system, but simply a rough indicator, as many factors other than temperature also play an important part where hardiness is concerned. These factors include altitude, wind exposure, proximity to water, soil type, the presence of snow or shade, night temperature, and the amount of water received by a plant. These kinds of factors can easily alter a plant's hardiness by as much as two zones. The presence of long-term snow cover in the winter especially can allow plants to survive in colder zones.

KEY TO ZONES

	Zone 1	Below -45°C (-50°F)
	Zone 2	-45 to -40°C (-50 to -40°F)
	Zone 3	-40 to -34°C (-40 to -30°F)
	Zone 4	-34 to -29°C (-30 to -20°F)
	Zone 5	-29 to -23°C (-20 to -10°F)
	Zone 6	-23 to -18°C (-10 to 0°F)
	Zone 7	-18 to -12°C (0 to 10°F)
	Zone 8	-12 to -7°C (10 to 20°F)
	Zone 9	-7 to -1°C (20 to 30°F)
	Zone 10	-1 to 4°C (30 to 40°F)
	Zone 11	Above 4°C (40°F)

ACKNOWLEDGEMENTS

Many thanks to the companies and individuals who allowed us to take photographs in their gardens: Tony and Gillian Adams, Coxheath, Kent; Ann Adey, Normandy Community Therapy Gardens, near Guildford; Capel Manor College, Middlesex; Thrive Trunkwell Garden, near Reading, Berkshire; Elizabeth Morris and Mary Clegg, Dorset; Connie and Joy Coote, Foster House (Beach Studios), Kent; Pat and Maureen Sidders, Wittisham; Sue Martin, Brickwall Cottage Nursery, Frittenden; and Ann Frazier and Alice Turowski, Portland Oregon, USA.

Many thanks to the models who kindly gave us their time: Tony and Gillian Adams; Jean Braban; Sue and Geoff Bylett; Bob Cooke; Connie and John Coote; Marie Cornish; David Dedrick; Heather Earl; Harry and Greta Freeman; Edward and Judith Grigg; Dorothy Hope; Brian Jenna; Keith Jenner; Sandy Marshall; Alan Martin; Leila and Peter Mellor; Fred Paine; Allen and Daphne Pincott; Hilda and Stuart Pratt; Mr and Mrs Rose; Pat and Maureen Sidders; Jim Smith; Neil and Mona

Warwick; Frank Wenham; Sylvia Winwood; Michael Wood; Peter and Barbara who put up the raspberry agriframe; Sylvia, Erica, Alan and Daphne from The Canterbury Oast Trust, Woodchurch, Kent; Ann, Marilyn, Bernard and Leslie from the Wednesday group at Capel Manor, Middlesex; Keith, Michael and Jean from St Michael's Hospice, St Leonards-on-Sea, East Sussex; and an extra special thanks to Sue Martin who helped throughout the shoot.

The publishers would also like to thank the following agencies and individuals for permission to reproduce their images: **Alamy:** p8t A Room with Views, p19tr Blickwinkel, p44b John Glover, p60tl Allan Bergmann Jensen, p217b Cubolmages srl, p221tr Cubolmages srl; **Adrian Burke:** p6b; **Patty Cassidy:** p96 middle col, p176b; **Felicity Forster:** p154b & p155; **Gap Photos:** p13bm Ron Evans, p19b Matt Anker, p31t Graham Strong, p34t Lynn Keddie, p34br Gerald Majumdar, p38br S & O, p39br Friedrich Strauss, p41bl Jonathan Buckley, p55br Leigh Clapp, p56tm Linda Burgess, p58t Gap Photos, p102t Dave Bevan, p127tr Gap Photos, p135tr Elke Borkowski, p164bl

Friedrick Strauss, p165b Lynn Keddie, p168t Jonathan Buckley, p208b Victoria Firmston, p211m BBC Magazines Ltd, p215b Jonathan Buckley, p218t Pernilla Bergdahl, p219b Dave Zubraski, p220t Howard Rice, p223b Jenny Lilly, p224b Dave Bevan, p225b J. S. Sira, p227t John Glover, p228t J. S. Sira, p228b Carole Drake, p229t John Glover, p230tl Martin Hughes-Jones, p232t Howard Rice, p232b Geoff Kidd, p235tr Maxine Adcock, p237b Pernilla Bergdahl, p238m Jonathan Buckley, p240t FhF Greenmedia, p241b Paul Debois, p243t John Glover, p246t Fiona McLeod, p248l Friedrick Strauss, p248m Maddie Thornhill, p249b John Glover; **Garden Picture Library:** p16bl Jason Ingram, p40bl Anne Green, p135b Friedrich Strauss, p159 Georgia Glynn Smith, p247t Andrew Lord; **Garden World Images:** p135tl Jacque Dracup, p209b Gilles Delacroix, p221tl Jenny Lilly, p231 Gilles Delacroix; **Robert Highton:** p126tr; **istock:** p15, p32, p39cl, p39 centre 2nd right, p39bl, p55t, p112bl, p112br, p142tl, p157t & br, p210t; **Claire Rae:** 138br; **Lynn Morton** p27t.